D1567466

# The Lost Journals of Nikola Tesla
## HAARP - Chemtrails
## and the Secret of Alternative 4

### By Tim Swartz

# Global Communications

THE LOST JOURNALS OF NIKOLA TESLA
HAARP - Chemtrails and the
Secret of Alternative 4
All Rights Reserved - Copyright © Global Communications
● ● ● ● ● ● ● ● ● ● ● ● ● ● ● ● ● ● ● ● ● ● ● ● ● ●

Cover art copyright Charles Gregory

6/01

ISBN: 1-892062-13-5
New Age/Occult/Technology

==================================================

==================================================

Written by Tim Swartz

Timothy G. Beckley, Editor Director
Carol Rodriguez, Publisher's Assistant

Free catalog from Global Communications,
Box 753, New Brunswick, NJ 08903
www.conspiracyjournal.com
Free subscription to CONSPIRACY JOURNAL
e-mailed every week. Go to above site NOW.

## The Lost Journals of Nikola Tesla

# Contents

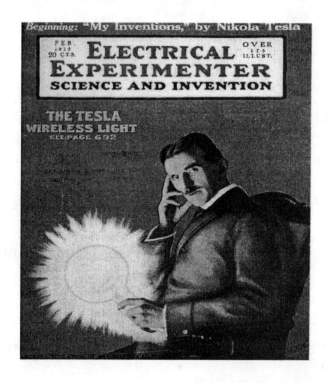

## Dedicated To My Wife

# The Lost Journals of Nikola Tesla

## INTRODUCTION
### By Timothy Green Beckley

There is a teacher named John W. Wagner who thinks that the Smithsonian Institute is playing favorites. After studying the remarkable life of Nikola Tesla, Wagner, along with his third grade class, started a campaign to educate the world about the obscure electrical genius from Yugoslavia.

Wagner and his class wrote many letters to important people asking for their support. A former student persuaded her father, an accomplished sculptor, to create a bust of Tesla for their class.

A Third Grade requirement is to learn cursive handwriting, so their class work now had a purpose...writing letters to raise money for their Tesla bust. Unfortunately, most people had never heard of Nikola Tesla. And those who had, seemed not to want to listen.

In fact, when the bust of Tesla was finished, Wagner and his class of eager students offered it to the Smithsonian Institute in Washington, DC. Dr. Bernard S. Finn, (Curator of the Division of Electricity and Modern Physics) refused, claiming he had no use for the bust.

They could not understand why the Smithsonian would have no use for a $6,000 bust of such a great American and world-class scientist. After all, Tesla was no slouch. Much of our modern technology owes its beginnings to Tesla. In 1882 he made the discovery that changed the world ! harnessing the awesome power of Alternating Current (AC).

In 1888 Tesla obtained U.S. patents covering an entire system of polyphase AC that remains unchanged in principle today. Tesla then promptly sold all of his patents to George Westinghouse, an acquisition that made the Westinghouse Company the giant it is today.

Westinghouse and Tesla were consummate friends, but after Westinghouse died in1913, the company forgot about its chief benefactor and Tesla fell victim to hard times. Tesla died January 7, 1943, alone, and all but forgotten, in a New York hotel room, paid for by a meager stipend provided by the Yugoslavian government.

Today, industries prosper and flourish, the world surges from the power his fertile mind created, radios blare with news and music, their transmission made possible by his great intellect, all telling us that the forgotten genius, Nikola Tesla, was here.

# The Lost Journals of Nikola Tesla

Tesla is preceded in greatness only by Michael Faraday who in 1831 rocked the scientific world with his discovery that magnetism can produce electricity, if it is accompanied by motion.

Faraday discovered the principle, but not how to make it power the world; Tesla alone accomplished this singular feat. Tesla is one of only two Americans to have a unit of electrical measurement named in his honor. Names for units of electrical measurement are derived by using the names of scientists who made the greatest contributions in electrical science, forming perhaps the most elite group in the world.

Throughout the entire history of electrical science only fifteen men worldwide have received this honor. Tesla is one of these great men. In addition, Tesla received fifteen honorary degrees from famous universities worldwide, including Yale and Columbia in the United States.

He also received fourteen Awards of Merit from other world class groups.

Dr. David L. Goodstein, Vice Provost and Professor of Physics at California Institute of Technology, calls Tesla one of the "Saints of Science" and equates him to Leonardo Da Vinci.

Tesla is the greatest inventor the world has ever forgotten. He is also the greatest inventor the Smithsonian has swept under the carpet. The Smithsonian's curator essentially credits Edison for our worldwide system of electricity. He also credits Marconi for the invention of radio.

This is a deliberate assault on factual history and needs to be challenged. The United States Patent Office and the U.S. Supreme Court view things a little differently over the much distorted history the Smithsonian publicizes.

Tesla holds over forty U.S. patents (circa 1888) covering our entire system of Polyphase Alternating Current (AC). These patents are so novel that nobody could ever challenge them in the courts.

The Direct Current (DC) system Edison used in his much touted Pearl Street generating station was invented by others before his time; he merely copied the work of others to promote his business enterprise. . . and the Smithsonian wants you to believe he was America's 'King of Electricity.'

There is simply no evidence to support this claim. The U.S. Supreme Court, in a landmark decision dated June 21, 1943, Case No. 369, overturned Marconi's basic patent for the invention of radio because Tesla's patent on the four-tuned circuit predated Marconi's patent. Marconi had simply copied Tesla's work.

# The Lost Journals of Nikola Tesla

Tesla's four-tuned circuits two on the receiving side and two on the transmitting side, secured by U.S. patents #645,576 and #649,621) were the basis of the U.S. Supreme Court decision (Case #369 decided June 21, 1943) to overturn Marconi's basic patent on the invention of radio.

Marconi merely demonstrated Tesla's invention, but the gullible media and the greedy industry that followed perpetuate a myth that Marconi invented radio. Who do you believe has more credibility. . . the industries that promote their own businesses, or the U.S. Supreme Court?

Marconi's two-tuned circuit system was the same as that advanced by Heinrich Hertz and was no more a viable system of radio than that advanced by Mahlon Loomis in 1872. . . long before Hertz or Tesla.

If you visit the Smithsonian, next to Edison's bust you will see Tesla's invention that revolutionized the world – drawing of Tesla's rotating magnetic field device, giving us polyphase AC and the AC motor.

Tesla's U.S. patent number is on his invention, but you wont find any recognition for Tesla. When Dr. Bernard S. Finn was asked why he had placed Edison's bust on display next to Tesla's invention, he said the sculptor was a phrenologist and wanted to examine the bumps on Edison's head; this made it authentic.

Edison used Direct Current (DC), a technology invented and developed by others, before his time, as a means of powering his incandescent lamp. Big business and the media have exaggerated this story so much that now everyone believes Edison is the father of our system of electrical power.

The Smithsonian Book of Invention is an extra-large hardcover book almost 7/8 of an inch thick. Many inventors and their inventions are shown and their impact on civilization discussed – including Edison, Marconi, Archie Bunker, and Colonel Sanders. Tesla and his epic-causing discoveries are omitted.

Dr. Bernard S. Finn is Curator and first author of this Smithsonian publication. In his section entitled: *The Beginning of the Electrical Age*, he names forty-three contributors to the science of electricity. Mr. Edison's name is cited many times along with his photographs, but Nikola Tesla's name is omitted.

Equally outrageous is the Niagara Falls power station picture of Tesla's AC generators on the last page. . .and Dr. Finn's concluding remark: "When the Niagara Falls power station began operating in 1895, it signaled the final major act in the revolutionary drama that began in Menlo Park in the fall of 1879."

# The Lost Journals of Nikola Tesla

By this time the totally brainwashed reader is led to believe that our electrical world started with Mr. Edison at Menlo Park, and then he finished electrifying America in1895 by creating the Niagara Falls power station. Yet it was Tesla's U.S. patents that were used in that power plant's creation and Edison had no role in the project.

Edison actually fought the adoption of AC bitterly by waging his infamous War of the Currents, culminating in his creation of the first electric chair in an attempt to frighten people away from the use of Tesla's AC system of electricity.

Despite attempts to relegate Tesla to the back pages of history, there has been a growing wave of interest in the man and his great works. Some of this interest stems from Tesla's comments made in his later years concerning exotic inventions and fantastic tales of Death Rays and communicating with extraterrestrials.

It is now known that various governments were extremely interested in Tesla's ideas for weapons and limitless energy. So much so that after his death, the U.S. military confiscated boxes full of Tesla's research and writings.

Much of this material has never been revealed to the public. What is not so widely known is that Tesla often suffered from financial difficulties, forcing him to move from hotel to hotel as his debt increased. Many times Tesla had to move, leaving crates of his belongings behind. The hotels would hold on to Tesla's possessions for awhile, but would eventually have to auction them off in order to repay Tesla's outstanding bills.

Often these sold off boxes contained notes outlining some new invention or speculations on developing technology. How much was lost over the years no one will ever know. However, some material escaped the clutches of obscurity and has recently resurfaced after being separated and stored for decades.

This new book examines some of this lost science, as well as shocking new details of Tesla's life as written by himself in long forgotten notes. These explosive journals, if true, could show that Tesla was indeed the first man to receive communications from life forms not of this planet!

These communications so frightened Tesla that he spent the remaining years of his life secretly dedicated to discovering the true purpose of the alleged extraterrestrials – and devising new technologies to enable mankind to protect itself from possible enslavement from a race of creatures that once called Earth home, and humankind their children.

Timothy Green Beckley

# The Lost Journals of Nikola Tesla

"We are whirling through endless space, with an inconceivable speed, all around us everything is spinning, everything is moving, everywhere there is energy. There must be some way of availing ourselves of this energy more directly. Then, with the light obtained from the medium, with the power derived from it, with every form of energy obtained without effort, from the store forever inexhaustible, humanity will advance with giant strides. The mere contemplation of these magnificent possibilities expands our minds, strengthens our hopes and fills our hearts with supreme delight."

Nikola Tesla, 1891

# Chapter One
### *The Secret Life Of Nikola Tesla*

Nikola Tesla was beyond a doubt the greatest genius of the 20th century. Our way of life today, the technology that we take for granted, is all possible because of this one incredible man from Europe.

However, despite all of his contributions to science, his name is little remembered outside the field of electronics and physics. In fact, Thomas Edison is often mistakenly credited in school textbooks with inventions that were developed and patented by Tesla.

Most scholars acknowledge that Tesla's obscurity is partially due to his eccentric ways and fantastic claims during the waning years of his life, of communicating with other planets and death rays. It is now known that many of these fantastic inventions of Tesla are scientifically accurate and workable. It has simply taken mankind this long to catch up to the astonishing ideas of a man who died in 1943.

It is known that Tesla suffered from financial troubles throughout his adult life. Because of this, Tesla had to move several times when he could no longer afford his surroundings. The Waldorf Astoria in New York had been Tesla's residence for twenty years, yet he had to move in 1920 when he could no longer afford it. Tesla then moved into the Hotel St. Regis, but again was forced to vacate due to lack of financial support.

Forced to move from hotel to hotel, he would often leave trunks of documents behind as security for his debts. These trunks, which were eagerly sought after Tesla's death, have become the key to unlocking the mystery of who Nikola Tesla really was, and the incredible life that he secretly lead.

When Tesla died on January 7, 1943 at the age of 86, representatives of the Office of Alien Property, at the request of the FBI, went to the Hotel New Yorker and seized all of Tesla's belongings. Two truckloads of papers, furniture and artifacts were sent under seal to the Manhattan Storage and Warehouse Company.

This load was added to the almost thirty barrels and bundles that had been in storage since the 1930's, and the entire collection was sealed under orders from the OAP. Strange behavior, considering that Tesla was a legal American citizen.

# The Lost Journals of Nikola Tesla

## The Forgotten Papers of Nikola Tesla

After Tesla's death, there was a scramble by the United States government to find all of his papers, notes and research before other foreign powers could find them. Tesla's nephew, Sava Kosanovic, reported that before the OAP had arrived, someone else had obviously gone through Tesla's belongings and took an unknown amount of personal notes and papers.

It was known by the FBI that German intelligence had already spirited away a sizable amount of Tesla's research several years before his death. This stolen material, it is thought, would eventually result in the development of the Nazi flying saucer. The United States was going to make sure that this would not happen again.

Anything even remotely associated with the great man was quickly confiscated and lost within the secret networks of pre-World War II America. Nevertheless, more than a dozen boxes of Tesla's belongings left behind at hotels like the Waldorf Astoria, the Governor Clinton Hotel and the St. Regis had already been sold to salvagers to pay off Tesla's outstanding bills.

Most of these boxes and the secrets they contained have never been found. In 1976, four undistinguished boxes of papers were auctioned in the estate sale of one Michael P. Bornes. Little is known about Bornes except that he had been a bookseller in Manhattan. This auction took place in Newark, NJ, with the boxes and their contents being bought by Dale Alfrey for twenty five dollars.

Alfrey had no idea what was in the boxes when he bought them on a whim. When he later went through them, he was surprised to find what appeared to be lab documents and personal notes of Nikola Tesla. Some of the lost papers of Tesla had once again resurfaced. However, due to ignorance they were almost lost once again.

In 1976, the name Nikola Tesla was not widely known. Alfrey had little idea of the importance of the papers he now owned. Going through the incredible amount of material, Alfrey at first thought he had uncovered the notes of a science fiction writer. What he read was so incredible that it seemed impossible that any of it was true.

Having little interest in what he had bought, Alfrey stashed the boxes away in his basement thinking that he would go through them again later when he had more time. Twenty years passed before Alfrey would once again find the time to open the strange boxes. Unfortunately, time had not been so kind to the precious contents contained within.

The papers by now had mildewed badly and the ink had faded from the years of neglect in the damp basement. Alfrey was determined not to let this material disappear forever and started the laborious effort of trying to transcribe the information before it was too late.

However, Alfrey soon found himself caught up in reading the remarkable papers. Tesla's notes are shocking in their revelations of the scientist's secret life. A life, that up until this time, had never been mentioned by Tesla, or documented by biographers after his death.

These lost journals revealed that in 1899, while in Colorado Springs, Tesla intercepted communications from extraterrestrial beings who were secretly controlling mankind. These creatures were slowly preparing humans for eventual conquest and domination, using a program that had been in place since the creation of humankind, but was now accelerating due to Earth's increased scientific awareness.

Tesla wrote about his years of research to interpret the strange radio signals, and his attempts to notify the government and military concerning what he had learned, but his letters apparently went unanswered.

Tesla spoke in confidence to several of his benefactors, including Colonel John Jacob Astor, who owned the Waldorf Astoria hotel. These benefactors listened to Tesla and secretly funded what was to be the start of mankind's first battle to regain control of its own destiny. A battle set in motion by Nikola Tesla.

While this information seems absolutely incredible, Tesla did give occasional hints to his predicament in various newspaper and magazine interviews. Tesla may have elaborated on the subject in an article called: *Talking With the Planets,* in *Colliers Weekly* (March 1901).

"As I was improving my machines for the production of intense electrical actions, I was also perfecting the means for observing feeble efforts. One of the most interesting results, and also one of great practical importance, was the development of certain contrivances for indicating at a distance of many hundred miles an approaching storm, its direction, speed and distance traveled.

"It was in carrying on this work that for the first time I discovered those mysterious effects which have elicited such unusual interest. I had perfected the apparatus referred to so far that from my laboratory in the Colorado mountains

# The Lost Journals of Nikola Tesla

I could feel the pulse of the globe, as it were, noting every electrical change that occurred within a radius of eleven hundred miles. I can never forget the first sensations I experienced when it dawned upon me that I had observed something possibly of incalculable consequences to mankind.

"I felt as though I were present at the birth of a new knowledge or the revelation of a great truth. My first observations positively terrified me, as there was present in them something mysterious, not to say supernatural, and I was alone in my laboratory at night; but at that time the idea of these disturbances being intelligently controlled signals did not yet present itself to me.

"The changes I noted were taking place periodically and with such a clear suggestion of number and order that they were not traceable to any cause known to me. I was familiar, of course, with such electrical disturbances as are produced by the sun, Aurora Borealis, and earth currents, and I was as sure as I could be of any fact that these variations were due to none of these causes.

"The nature of my experiments precluded the possibility of the changes being produced by atmospheric disturbances, as has been rashly asserted by some. It was some time afterward when the thought flashed upon my mind that the disturbances I had observed might be due to an intelligent control. Although I could not decipher their meaning, it was impossible for me to think of them as having been entirely accidental.

"The feeling is constantly growing on me that I had been the first to hear the greeting of one planet to another. A purpose was behind these electrical signals."

Decades later on his birthday in 1937, he announced: "I have devoted much of my time during the year past to the perfecting of a new small and compact apparatus by which energy in considerable amounts can now be flashed through interstellar space to any distance without the slightest dispersion." (*New York Times*, Sunday, 11 July1937.)

Tesla never publicly revealed any technical details of his improved transmitter, but in his 1937 announcement, he revealed a new formula showing that: "The kinetic and potential energy of a body is the result of motion and determined by the product of its mass and the square of its velocity. Let the mass be reduced, the energy is reduced by the same proportion. If it be reduced to zero, the energy is likewise zero for any finite velocity." (*New York Sun*, 12 July 1937, p. 6.)

Why is it that there has been little written about Tesla's belief that he had listened in on alien radio signals? Perhaps the truth has been kept secret.

# The Lost Journals of Nikola Tesla

## The Men-In-Black Pay a Visit

By the summer of 1997, Alfrey had finished reading the entire contents of the four boxes and was ready to start scanning the papers on to computer disks. Alfrey had been more than a little surprised that the voluminous notes and journals contained no drawings or blueprints. It was not until later that Alfrey discovered that Tesla detested illustrating his ideas owing to the fact that his own mental blueprints were all that he required to build his inventions.

Alfrey also noticed that Tesla's journals were often incomplete. There were numerous gaps consisting of days, months and even years. Alfrey surmised that other journals could exist somewhere, hidden away either by the government, or by ignorance in forgotten warehouses and attics.

Because of these gaps, Alfrey started to make inquiries over the Internet hoping that others may have additional information concerning the missing sections. These inquiries obviously attracted the attentions of those who were also interested in the lost journals. Someone who wanted the journals to remain lost forever.

In September 1997, Alfrey was home continuing his research while his wife and children were gone for the day to Manhattan. As Alfrey remembers, the phone rang and the caller identified himself as Jay Kowski who was interested in Tesla and the papers that Alfrey had discovered.

Alfrey had spoken to the caller for only a few minutes when suddenly the line went dead. Almost immediately the front door bell rang, Alfrey recalled. "When I went to answer the front door, I found it already open with three men standing in the foyer."

Before Alfrey could speak, the man closest addressed him by his first name. "The door was open John, I hope you don't mind that we let ourselves in?"

The three men were all dressed in identical black business suits with white shirts and black ties. "They looked just like undertakers,"Alfrey said.

However, Alfrey could tell that these men were not undertakers, or simply there for a friendly chat. The man who had first spoken continued to address Alfrey by his first name: "Like he knew me personally or something. But I had never seen these men before in my life. I was afraid that maybe they were criminals. There was a palatable air of menace around these three that I had never experienced before, or after."

The other two men remained close to the door and never spoke. Their eyes remained fixed on Alfrey throughout the entire experience.

"We understand that you have in your possession some old boxes and papers," the first man said. "We would be very interested in buying these from you."

"Well, they're not really for sale,"Alfrey answered. "Anyway, how do you know about them?"

The first man chuckled. "We know a lot about you and your papers. They don't belong to you, but we would be willing to pay you for your troubles. They're of no use to you, in fact, you could be in a lot of trouble for having them in the first place."

By now, Alfrey realized that the men were not asking to buy his boxes, they were demanding them. He could tell that they meant business and this frightened him.

The first man now slowly moved closer to Alfrey, speaking in a slow deliberate way. He carefully enunciated each word so that Alfrey understood perfectly where he stood.

"Its no use you know, the man said. Were going to get these boxes no matter what you do. You can't stop us. It would be much easier for you and your family if you just gave us what we want. People have disappeared forever over much less than this. I would so hate to see this happen to you, or your wife and kids."

The man now stood directly in front of Alfrey, his dark eyes fixed and cold. It almost seemed that they had some kind of hypnotic power over Alfrey as he stood there unable to speak.

Suddenly, all three of the strange men turned in unison and walked out the front door. Nothing further was said, it wasn't necessary, Alfrey understood their message clearly. He was to give up the boxes, his research, even his interest in Tesla if he wanted to remain out of harms way.

It was as if Alfrey was coming out of a trance, he realized what had happened and he rushed out the door to confront the men. But, they were nowhere to be seen. There was no car in the driveway and the street was completely empty. In fact, the entire neighborhood was eerily quiet. Even the birds had fallen silent. It was as if the world had paused for a moment, then continued on as if nothing had happened.

Alfrey rushed back into his house and locked the doors. He then went into his study where he kept the boxes and computer. The room was located at the back of the house and had no separate entrance to the outside. It obviously wasn't needed, because all four boxes, the papers contained within and the computer disks were now all gone.

It was obvious that the three men were only a distraction while someone else silently entered the house and ransacked the study, removing everything that pertained to Nikola Tesla. This included separate books and magazine articles that Alfrey had collected while he was doing research on the matter.

Worse yet, not only were his papers missing, but his computer hard drive had been completely erased. Everything that he had on it, including items not related to Tesla, were destroyed.

All evidence that he had on Tesla and his missing journals were now gone forever. Alfrey refused to speak about his frightening incident for several months. He told no one what had happened, not even his wife. It was as if he was in a state of mental shock that perpetually clouded his mind.

Slowly he began to regain his senses and remember the details of that day. He recalled that the three men dressed exactly alike, were almost the same height, and all three had their hair cut short with odd looking long bangs that covered their foreheads.

The three men also had unnatural looking tanned skin. Almost like they had used a bottled tanner that dyes the skin a dark brown. Other than these peculiarities, the men appeared to be normal. It had not occurred to Alfrey that they could be something other than what they seemed. It was not until later, when relating this strange story that someone remarked about the MIBs.

Alfrey had never heard about the Men-In-Black. He had heard about the movie, but had not made the connection. After doing a little research and reading several books by the authors John Keel and Commander X, Alfrey was certain that he had received a visit from the Men-In-Black, or at least someone who wanted to look like the Men-In-Black.

This is where Dale Alfrey's strange story comes to an end. Everything that he had done connected to Nikola Tesla has been taken away from him. Fortunately, due to his spending hours reading the Tesla papers, he has retained a good memory of their contents. Not a perfect recollection, but sufficient to relate for this book.

Alfrey wonders if his boxes were the last of the missing belongings of Tesla. Or could others still remain forgotten somewhere, waiting to be rediscovered.

# The Lost Journals of Nikola Tesla

## What Tesla Believed

Newspaper articles from the time of Tesla's death relate that possibly over a dozen large boxes of Tesla's notes were never found by the government. These could still be out there somewhere, waiting for some lucky individual to rediscover their lost secrets.

It can only be speculated on what would be found inside other forgotten boxes of notes and personal belongings, possibly the missing information concerning Tesla's secret battle with the government and his knowledge of alien life forms.

The papers that Dale Alfrey found revealed a side of Tesla not known to the public. Tesla apparently had spent a number of years trying to translate the mysterious signals he first heard in 1899.

His basic interpretation of these signals was that creatures from another planet, "Martials" as the slang of the day called them, were secretly here on Earth - They had infiltrated humankind for centuries - They had controlled events and people in order to lead mankind on a path of evolutionary development and essentially were responsible for human's being on the planet in the first place.

As well, Tesla discovered that the planets overall temperature was slowly increasing, what we know today as global warming. Tesla thought that this was being brought about by natural conditions, as well as manmade and extraterrestrial interference.

With this in mind, we can now see some of the reasons for Tesla's eccentric behavior in the later years of his life. Tesla became obsessed with creating devices to end warfare and join mankind against what he perceived as the common enemy of extraterrestrials. He often spoke about "Death Rays" and "Wingless Torpedo's" that could fly through the air without propellers or jets, possibly one of the earliest mentions of flying saucers.

Tesla also became interested in developing methods to create free energy from sources other than burning wood or fossil fuels. Tesla was obviously the first to realize the dire consequences that could await us if the greenhouse effect was to take place.

Unfortunately, Tesla's attempts to elevate humankind with new technology were met with laughter and derision. His letters about his concerns, sent to his friends in the government, were ignored. Tesla must have felt that he knew the biggest secret in the world concerning the fate of mankind, and nobody cared.

# Chapter Two
## *Alien Signals in the Night*

### Excerpts From the personal memoirs of Nikola Tesla

The progressive development of man is vitally dependent on invention. It is the most important product of his creative brain. Its ultimate purpose is the complete mastery of mind over the material world, the harnessing of the forces of nature to human needs.

This is the difficult task of the inventor who is often misunderstood and unrewarded. But he finds ample compensation in the pleasing exercises of his powers and in the knowledge of being one of that exceptionally privileged class without whom the race would have long ago perished in the bitter struggle against pitiless elements. Speaking for myself, I have already had more than my full measure of this exquisite enjoyment; so much, that for many years my life was little short of continuous rapture.

I am credited with being one of the hardest workers and perhaps I am, if thought is the equivalent of labor, for I have devoted to it almost all of my waking hours. But if work is interpreted to be a definite performance in a specified time according to a rigid rule, then I may be the worst of idlers.

Every effort under compulsion demands a sacrifice of life-energy. I never paid such a price. On the contrary, I have thrived on my thoughts. In attempting to give a connected and faithful account of my activities in this story of my life, I must dwell, however reluctantly, on the impressions of my youth and the circumstances and events which have been instrumental in determining my career.

Our first endeavors are purely instinctive promptings of an imagination vivid and undisciplined. As we grow older, reason asserts itself and we become more and more systematic and designing. But those early impulses, though not immediately productive, are of the greatest moment and may shape our very destinies.

Indeed, I feel now that had I understood and cultivated instead of suppressing them, I would have added substantial value to my bequest to the world. But not until I had attained manhood did I realize that I was an inventor. This was due to a number of causes.

# The Lost Journals of Nikola Tesla

In the first place I had a brother who was gifted to an extraordinary degree; one of those rare phenomena of mentality which biological investigation has failed to explain. His premature and unexpected death left my parents disconsolate.

We owned a horse which had been presented to us by a dear friend. It was a magnificent animal of Arabian breed, possessed of almost human intelligence, and was cared for and petted by the whole family, having on one occasion saved my dear father's life under remarkable circumstances.

My father had been called one winter night to perform an urgent duty and while crossing the mountains, infested by wolves, the horse became frightened and ran away, throwing him violently to the ground.

It arrived home bleeding and exhausted, but after the alarm was sounded, immediately dashed off again, returning to the spot, and before the searching party were far on the way they were met by my father, who had recovered consciousness and remounted, not realizing that he had been lying in the snow for several hours.

This horse was responsible for my brother's injuries from which he died. I witnessed the tragic scene and although so many years have elapsed since, my visual impression of it has lost none of its force.

The recollection of his attainments made every effort of mine seem dull in comparison. Anything I did that was creditable merely caused my parents to feel their loss more keenly. So I grew up with little confidence in myself. But I was far from being considered a stupid boy, if I am to judge from an incident of which I still have a strong remembrance.

One day the Aldermen were passing through a street where I was playing with other boys. The oldest of these venerable gentlemen, a wealthy citizen, paused to give a silver piece to each of us. Coming to me, he suddenly stopped and commanded, "Look in my eyes."

I met his gaze, my hand outstretched to receive the much valued coin, when to my dismay, he said, "No, not much; you can get nothing from me. You are too smart."

My mother descended from one of the oldest families in the country and a line of inventors. Both her father and grandfather originated numerous implements for household, agricultural and other uses. She was a truly great woman, of rare skill, courage and fortitude. I owe so much to her good graces and inventive mind that I can still today see her wonderful features etched upon my mind.

# The Lost Journals of Nikola Tesla

## The Inner Mind Made Real

In my boyhood I suffered from a peculiar affliction due to the appearance of images, often accompanied by strong flashes of light, which marred the sight of real objects and interfered with my thoughts and action. They were pictures of things and scenes which I had really seen, never of those imagined.

When a word was spoken to me the image of the object it designated would present itself vividly to my vision and sometimes I was quite unable to distinguish whether what I saw was tangible or not.

This caused me great discomfort and anxiety. None of the students of psychology or physiology whom I have consulted, could ever explain satisfactorily these phenomenon.

They seem to have been unique although I was probably predisposed as I know that my brother experienced a similar trouble. The theory I have formulated is that the images were the result of a reflex action from the brain on the retina under great excitation. They certainly were not hallucinations such as are produced in diseased and anguished minds, for in other respects I was normal and composed.

To give an idea of my distress, suppose that I had witnessed a funeral or some such nerve-wracking spectacle. Then, inevitably, in the stillness of night, a vivid picture of the scene would thrust itself before my eyes and persist despite all my efforts to banish it from my innermost being.

I also began to see visions of things that bore no resemblance to reality. It was as if I was being shown ideas of some cosmic mind, waiting to make real its conceptions.

If my explanation is correct, it should be possible to project on a screen the image of any object one conceives and make it visible. Such an advance would revolutionize all human relations. I am convinced that this wonder can and will be accomplished in time to come.

I may add that I have devoted much thought to the solution of the problem. I have managed to reflect such a picture, which I have seen in my mind, to the mind of another person, in another room.

To free myself of these tormenting appearances, I tried to concentrate my mind on something else I had seen, and in this way I would often obtain temporary relief; but in order to get it I had to conjure continuously new images.

# The Lost Journals of Nikola Tesla

It was not long before I found that I had exhausted all of those at my command; my "reel" had run out as it were, because I had seen little of the world - only objects in my home and the immediate surroundings.

As I performed these mental operations for the second or third time, in order to chase the appearances from my vision, the remedy gradually lost all its force. Then instinctively commenced to make excursions beyond the limits of the small world of which I had knowledge, and I saw new scenes.

These were at first very blurred and indistinct, and would flit away when I tried to concentrate my attention upon them. They gained in strength and distinctness and finally assumed the concreteness of real things.

I soon discovered that my best comfort was attained if I simply went on in my vision further and further, getting new impressions all the time, and so I began to travel; of course, in my mind. Every night, (and sometimes during the day), when alone, I would start on my journeys, see new places, cities and countries; live there, meet people and make friendships and acquaintances and, however unbelievable, it is a fact that they were just as dear to me as those in actual life, and not a bit less intense in their manifestations.

This I did constantly until I was about seventeen, when my thoughts turned seriously to invention. Then I observed to my delight that I could visualize with the greatest facility. I needed no models, drawings or experiments. I could picture them all as real in my mind.

Thus I have been led unconsciously to evolve what I consider a new method of materializing inventive concepts and ideas, which is radially opposite to the purely experimental and is in my opinion ever so much more expeditious and efficient.

The moment one constructs a device to carry into practice a crude idea, he finds himself unavoidably engrossed with the details of the apparatus. As he goes on improving and reconstructing, his force of concentration diminishes and he loses sight of the great underlying principle.

Results may be obtained, but always at the sacrifice of quality. My method is different. I do not rush into actual work. When I get an idea, I start at once building it up in my imagination. I change the construction, make improvements and operate the device in my mind.

It is absolutely immaterial to me whether I run my turbine in thought or test it in my shop. I even note if it is out of balance. There is no difference whatever; the results are the same.

# The Lost Journals of Nikola Tesla

In this way I am able to rapidly develop and perfect a conception without touching anything. When I have gone so far as to embody in the invention every possible improvement I can think of and see no fault anywhere, I put into concrete form this final product of my brain. Invariably my device works as I conceived that it should, and the experiment comes out exactly as I planned it.

In twenty years there has not been a single exception. Why should it be otherwise? Engineering, electrical and mechanical, is positive in results. There is scarcely a subject that cannot be examined beforehand, from the available theoretical and practical data.

The carrying out into practice of a crude idea as is being generally done, is, I hold, nothing but a waste of energy, money, and time. My early affliction had however, another compensation. The incessant mental exertion developed my powers of observation and enabled me to discover a truth of great importance.

I had noted that the appearance of images was always preceded by actual vision of scenes under peculiar and generally very exceptional conditions, and I was impelled on each occasion to locate the original impulse.

After a while this effort grew to be almost automatic and I gained great facility in connecting cause and effect. Soon I became aware, to my surprise, that every thought I conceived was suggested by an external impression. Not only this but all my actions were prompted in a similar way.

In the course of time it became perfectly evident to me that I was merely an automation endowed with power of movement responding to the stimuli of the sense organs and thinking and acting accordingly.

The practical result of this was the art of "teleautomatics" which has been so far carried out only in an imperfect manner. Its latent possibilities will, however be eventually shown. I have been years planning self-controlled automata and believe that mechanisms can be produced which will act as if possessed of reason, to a limited degree, and will create a revolution in many commercial and industrial departments.

I was about twelve years of age when I first succeeded in banishing an image from my vision by willful effort, but I never had any control over the flashes of light to which I have referred. They were, perhaps, my strangest and [most] inexplicable experience.

They usually occurred when I found myself in a dangerous or distressing situation or when I was greatly exhilarated. In some instances I have seen all the air around me filled with tongues of living flame. Their intensity, instead of diminishing, increased with time and seemingly attained a maximum when I was about twenty-five years old.

While in Paris in 1883, a prominent French manufacturer sent me an invitation to a shooting expedition which I accepted. I had been long confined to the factory and the fresh air had a wonderfully invigorating effect on me.

On my return to the city that night, I felt a positive sensation that my brain had caught fire. I was a light as though a small sun was located in it and I passed the whole night applying cold compressions to my tortured head.

Finally the flashes diminished in frequency and force but it took more than three weeks before they wholly subsided. When a second invitation was extended to me, my answer was an emphatic NO!

These luminous phenomena still manifest themselves from time to time, as when anew idea opening up possibilities strikes me, but they are no longer exciting, being of relatively small intensity. When I close my eyes I invariably observe first, a background of very dark and uniform blue, not unlike the sky on a clear but starless night.

In a few seconds this field becomes animated with innumerable scintillating flakes of green, arranged in several layers and advancing towards me. Then there appears, to the right, a beautiful pattern of two systems of parallel and closely spaced lines, at right angles to one another, in all sorts of colors with yellow, green, and gold predominating.

Immediately thereafter, the lines grow brighter and the whole is thickly sprinkled with dots of twinkling light. This picture moves slowly across the field of vision and in about ten seconds vanishes on the left, leaving behind a ground of rather unpleasant and inert gray until the second phase is reached.

Every time, before falling asleep, images of persons or objects flit before my view. When I see them I know I am about to lose consciousness. If they are absent and refuse to come, it means a sleepless night.

During this period I contracted many strange likes, dislikes and habits, some of which I can trace to external impressions while others are unaccountable. I was fascinated with the glitter of crystals, but pearls would almost give me a fit.

After finishing the studies at the Polytechnic Institute and University, I had a complete nervous breakdown and, while the malady lasted, I observed many phenomena, strange and unbelievable.

# The Lost Journals of Nikola Tesla

## Nikola Tesla - Born July 9/10, 1856

From Tesla's own writings we can observe that he had a unique mental capacity that few of his fellow human beings have ever hoped to achieve. It is no wonder that when Tesla was faced with an event as mind-shaking as the revelation that humans may not be alone in the universe, he faced it head on.

Tesla's atypical way of facing and dealing with the unknown has lead some to speculate that his true parentage may have originated from beyond this planet. This suggestion is not new, in fact, Tesla once confided to one of his personal assistants that he often felt that he was a stranger to this world.

Tesla was from a family of Serbian origin. Born in the village of Smiljan, Lika (Austria-Hungary) in what is now Croatia. Tesla's father was an Orthodox priest; his mother was unschooled but highly intelligent. A dreamer with a poetic touch, as he matured Tesla added to these earlier qualities those of self-discipline and a desire for precision.

Margaret Cheney, in her book: *Tesla: Man out of time* (1981), noted that Tesla as a child began to make original inventions. When he was five, he built a small waterwheel quite unlike those he had seen in the countryside. It was smooth, without paddles, yet it spun evenly in the current. Years later he was to recall this fact when designing his unique bladeless turbine.

Some of his other experiments were less successful. Once he perched on the roof of the barn, clutching the family umbrella and hyperventilating on the fresh mountain breeze until his body felt light and the dizziness in his head convinced him he could fly. Plunging to earth, he lay unconscious and was carried off to bed by his mother. Tesla would later write that this incident was the catalysis for his unusual visions.

In her book *Return of the Dove*, Margaret Storm states that Tesla was not an earth man. On page 71 of her privately printed book, she says that the space people related that a male child was born on board a spaceship which was on a flight from Venus to the earth in July, 1856.

The little boy was called Nikola. The ship landed at midnight, between July 9 and 10, in a remote mountain province in what is now Croatia. There, according to prior arrangements, the child was placed in the care of a good man and his wife, the Rev. Milutin and Djouka Tesla. Supposedly, the space people released this information in 1947 to Arthur H. Matthews of Quebec, Canada.

# The Lost Journals of Nikola Tesla

## Alien Signals in the Night

Arthur H. Matthews was an electrical engineer who from boyhood was closely associated with Tesla. Matthews claimed that Tesla entrusted him with many tasks, including the Tesla interplanetary communications set that was first conceived in 1901, with the objective of communicating with the planet Mars. Tesla had suggested that he could transmit through the earth and air, great amounts of power to distances of thousands of miles.

"I can easily bridge the gulf which separates us from Mars, and send a message almost as easily as to Chicago." Due to pressures of other research at the time, the first working model was not built by Tesla until 1918.

In 1899, Nikola Tesla, with the aid of his financial backer, J.P. Morgan, set up at Colorado Springs an experimental laboratory containing high voltage radio transmission equipment. The lab had a 200 ft. tower for transmission and reception of radio waves and the best receiving equipment available at the time.

One night, when he was alone in the laboratory, Tesla observed what he cautiously referred to as electrical actions which definitely appeared to be intelligent signals. The changes were taking place periodically and with such a clear suggestion of number and order that they could not be traced to any cause then known to him.

Tesla elaborated on the subject of *Talking With the Planets* in *Collier's Weekly* (March 1901): "As I was improving my machines for the production of intense electrical actions, I was also perfecting the means for observing feeble efforts. One of the most interesting results, and also one of great practical importance, was the development of certain contrivances for indicating at a distance of many hundred miles an approaching storm, its direction, speed and distance traveled.

"It was in carrying on this work that for the first time I discovered those mysterious effects which have elicited such unusual interest. I had perfected the apparatus referred to so far that from my laboratory in the Colorado mountains I could feel the pulse of the globe, as it were, noting every electrical change that occurred within a radius of eleven hundred miles.

"I can never forget the first sensations I experienced when it dawned upon me that I had observed something possibly of incalculable consequences to mankind. I felt as though I were present at the birth of a new knowledge or the revelation of a great truth...My first observations positively terrified me, as there was present in them something mysterious, not to say supernatural, and I was alone in my laboratory at night; but at that time the idea of these disturbances being intelligently controlled signals did not yet present itself to me.

"The changes I noted were taking place periodically and with such a clear suggestion of number and order that they were not traceable to any cause known to me. I was familiar, of course, with such electrical disturbances as are produced by the sun, Aurora Borealis, and earth currents, and I was as sure as I could be of any fact that these variations were due to none of these causes.

"The nature of my experiments precluded the possibility of the changes being produced by atmospheric disturbances, as has been rashly asserted by some. It was sometime afterward when the thought flashed upon my mind that the disturbances I had observed might be due to an intelligent control.

"Although I could not at the time decipher their meaning, it was impossible for me to think of them as having been entirely accidental. The feeling is constantly growing on me that I had been the first to hear the greeting of one planet to another. A purpose was behind these electrical signals"

This incident was the first of many in which Tesla intercepted what he felt were intelligent signals from space. At the time, it was surmised by prominent scientists that Mars would be a likely haven for intelligent life in our solar system, and Tesla at first thought these signals may be originating from the red planet. He would later change this viewpoint as he became more adept at translating the mysterious signals. Near the end of his life, Tesla had developed several inventions that allegedly could send powerful amounts of energy to other planets.

In 1937, during one of his birthday press conferences, Tesla announced: "I have devoted much of my time over the years to the perfecting of a new small and compact apparatus by which energy in considerable amounts can now be flashed through interstellar space to any distance without the slightest dispersion." (*New York Times*, July 11, 1937.)

Tesla never publicly revealed the technical details of his improved transmitter, but in his 1937 announcement, he revealed a new formula showing that "The kinetic and potential energy of a body is the result of motion and determined by the product of its mass and the square of its velocity. Let the mass be reduced, the energy is reduced by the same proportion. If it be reduced to zero, the energy is likewise zero for any finite velocity." (*New York Sun*, July 12, 1937, pg. 6.)

# *The Lost Journals of Nikola Tesla*

## A Fear of Aliens

In the Tesla journals that he uncovered, Dale Alfrey noted that by the 1920's Tesla had grown confident that he was able to make sense of the strange radio broadcasts from space. However, soon afterwards, Tesla began to expressed great concerns about beings from other planets who had unsavory designs for planet Earth.

"The signals are too strong to have traveled the great distances from Mars to Earth," wrote Tesla. "So I am forced to admit to myself that the sources must come from somewhere in nearby space or even the moon. I am certain however, that the creatures that communicate with each other every night are not from Mars, or possibly from any other planet in our solar system."

Several years after Tesla announced his reception of signals from space, Guglielmo Marconi also claimed to have heard from an alien radio transmitter. However, Marconi was just as quickly dismissed by his contemporaries, who claimed that he had received interference from another radio station on Earth.

There is some public confirmation in the validity of the lost journals and Tesla's belief in extraterrestrials and the importance of communicating with them. As noted earlier, Arthur H. Mathews claimed that Tesla had secretly developed the Teslascope for the purpose of communicating with aliens. The late Dr. Andrija Puharich interviewed Matthews for the *Pyramid Guide*, May-June & July-Aug. 1978. This interview revealed for the first time Matthews connections to Tesla.

Arthur Matthews was born in England and his father was a laboratory assistant to the noted physicist Lord Kelvin back in the 1890s. Tesla came over to England to meet Kelvin...to convince him that Alternating Current was more efficient than Direct Current. Kelvin at that time opposed the AC movement.

In 1902, the Matthews family left England and immigrated to Canada. When Matthews was 16 his father arranged for him to apprentice under Tesla. He eventually worked for him and continued this alliance until Tesla's death in 1943.

"It's not generally known, but Tesla actually had two huge magnifying transmitters built in Canada," Matthews said. "I operated one of them. People mostly know about the Colorado Springs transmitters and the unfinished one on Long Island. I saw the two Canadian transmitters. All the evidence is there."

Matthews stated that the Teslascope is the thing Tesla invented to communicate with beings on other planets. There's a diagram of the Teslascope in Matthews book, *The Wall of Light*. In principle, it takes in cosmic ray signals," Matthew's said. "Eventually the signals are stepped down to audio. Speak into one end, and the signal goes out the other end as a cosmic ray emitter."

Matthews' diagrams of the Teslascope make little electronic sense. No one has ever confirmed the reality of the device. Matthews claims, however, that he built a model Tesla Interplanetary Communications Set in 1947 and operated it successfully.

He suggested that due to the sets limited range, he was only able to contact spacecraft operating near the earth. He had hoped to someday build a set capable of communicating directly to the planets.

"Tesla had told me that beings from other planets were already here," related Matthews. "He was very afraid that they had been controlling man for thousands of years and that we were simply test subjects for an experiment of extremely long duration."

Matthews did not share in Tesla's convictions that aliens may not have the Earth's best interests in mind. His opinion was that if extraterrestrials were so advanced as to be able to travel from solar system to solar system, then they must also be socially advanced and peace-loving.

Matthews eagerness to continue experimenting with the Teslascope was indicative of the early days of the so-called "modern UFO era." By the 1950's, contactees such as George Adamski and Howard Menger were writing books and lecturing to eager believers about the almost god-like space brothers.

These UFO occupants claimed to be from almost every planet in the solar system, with Venus and Mars being especially favored. The space brothers preached a form of "New Age Space Religion," with utopian descriptions of their home worlds and denouncement of mankind's warlike ways.

Tesla would certainly have felt vindicated by his earlier claims if he had lived long enough to experience the modern UFO era. He mentions in his journals his frustrating attempts to interest those in the government or military about his theories. Apparently Tesla's letters went unanswered – the question remains whether or not his ideas were seriously considered or if he was thought of as simply a crackpot.

Circumstantial evidence points to a certain amount of expectation by the United States when the first UFOs were sighted during WWII. It could be that Tesla's ideas had more impact, albeit secretly, than Tesla ever imagined.

Nikola Tesla had suggested that he could transmit through the earth and air, great amounts of power to distances of thousands of miles. "I can easily bridge the gulf which separates us from Mars, and send a message almost as easily as to Chicago."

# Chapter Three
## Communicating With Other Planets

Robert A. Nelson in his article, *Communicating with Mars: The Experiments of Tesla & Hodowanec*, details the accidental communication with ET intelligences by L. G. Lawrence, the field manage of the ECOLA Institute. These communications could be the same types of signals received by Tesla at Colorado Springs in 1899.

On October 29, 1971, while conducting exploratory RBS [Remote Biological Sensing] experiments in Riverside County, California, the field organic transducer complex intercepted a train of apparently intelligent signals (tight spacing and discrete pulse intervals) while pointed at the constellation Ursa Major during a short rest period. The phenomenon continued for over 33 minutes.

A similar phenomenon was observed on April 10, 1972. The apparent signals, aside from growing weaker, appeared to be transmitted at great intervals ranging from weeks to months, possibly years. A faint, coherent, binary-type phenomenon was noted during aural monitoring. Intervals between rapid series of pulse trains ranged from three to ten minutes.

Because their equipment was shielded to electromagnetic radiation and found free of internal anomalies, the tentative conclusion of biological-type interstellar communications signals was favored.

Apparently the auditory part of the signal was unpleasant to hear, however, after multiple playbacks, the sound seemed to produce a type of enchantment to the listener. This was attributed to a psycho-acoustical adaptation.

The tape contained a short, incremental series of deep, harmonious oscillations resembling background modulations. An intelligent character of the overall pulse was applied by discrete spacing patterns, apparent repetitions of sequences, and highly attenuated Gaussian noise. (*Borderlands*, 1st Qtr., 1996, pp. 27-29).

Electrical engineer Greg Hodowanec has developed a theory of Rhysmonic Cosmology. He also experimented with a Gravity Wave Detector (GWD) of his own design. The simple devices detect "coherent modulations" in microwave radiation.

Hodowanec published his first report of *SETI with Gravitational Signals* using his GWDs (*Radio Astronomy*, April 1986): "The advantage of a possible gravitational technique for SETI over the radio technique is primarily one of time of 'propagation' for these signals. The radio waves travel at the speed of light, but the gravitational signals (per the writer's theories) are essentially instantaneous signals. Another advantage of the gravitational technique is the simplicity of the instrumentation required. As SARA members know, radio astronomy can be quite complicated.

"The gravitational wave detectors must rely largely on the Earth's mass as a 'shadow' to enable the detection of gravitational radiation. Therefore, 'objects' or signals located in the observers' zenith are best detected. Yet, the other areas are still 'detectable' especially with the aid of other 'shadows' such as the sun, moon, planets, etc.

"Of particular interest to SETI observers may be the strange audio type gravitational signals which appear to come from the Auriga and Perseus region of our Galaxy. These 'signals' have been 'heard' by the writer for several years now, and generally range between about four and five hours right ascension, with a peak intensity near 4.5 hours R.A. The signals appear to be several 'tones.'"

In a letter written to *Radio-Electronics Magazine* on July 23, 1988, Hodowanec mentions a definite contact with an extraterrestrial source: "On the morning of this date, at 7:30 to 7:38 AM (EST), I recorded the following apparently Morse-Code like pulses: A A A A R A R T T N N N N K C N N N E E E E E N E N N T T T N E E E E E A E E R K E N N E T E E A A A A E E E N T T K N T N T S E S E S E S E M N A S E S E S E S E S E S E S E S E —

"As you can see, these do not appear to be just random pulses, but the SE signals, which are most prevalent, appear to be possibly an identification signal. These signals are detected in shielded 1/f detectors and thus are scalar (gravitational) in nature.

"The signals above (if they were extraterrestrial) came from either the Auriga-Perseus region near my zenith or the Bootes region under my Earth position. I still cannot rule out that they may just be due to Earth core movements of some sort which are remarkably like Morse code signals, or even the possibility that they are man-made."

By July 1988, Hodowanec had confirmed Tesla's claims, as he announced in *Some Remarks on Tesla's Mars Signals*: "Such signals are being received today with simple modern-day scalar-type signal detectors...coherent modulations are being 'heard' in [the microwave] background radiation. The most prominent modulations being three pulses (code S) slightly separated in time, a la Tesla. On occasions, the code equivalents of an E, N, A, or K, are also heard, but the most persistent response is SE, SE, etc. Any 1/f type noise detector will respond to this background modulation. However, the experimenter must be careful that he is not creating these responses at the 'local' level by his own or other local actions.

"For example, the detectors will also respond to heart beats, breathing actions, local movements, as well as possible psychic effects. The detectors are easy to make and the experimenter should easily reproduce these results."

Further information by Hodowanec was released in a *Cosmology Data Note* (10-13-88): "Since about early August 1988, it was noticed that apparently 'intelligent signals' existed in these modulations [of the microwave background radiation]. It can be said that the intelligence was in the form of digital-type communication, e.g., dots and dashes, or ones and zeros.

"This type of communication may have been chosen by this 'unknown communicator' as it was conducive to the 'mass movement' form of longitudinal gravity signaling, as well as an easily recognizable universal system. This same method was proposed by the writer for a gravity system communication method.

"These 'signals' were noticed to be similar to the simpler International Morse Code symbols, primarily because they are the simplest way to present information in the pulse form. Thus, the 'letters' found in these transmissions are typically: E, I, T, M, A, N, R, K, S and O, as well as the comma and the wait signal. However, numbers are seen here as the simple series of pulses, e.g., 1 is one pulse, 2 is two pulses, 3 is three pulses, and so on.

"On August 26, 1988, after the writer had sent the message 'Greg Radio' during a local gravity signal transmission test, it was noticed that the letters G and D were apparently added to some of the received messages noted thereafter.

"The writer's first hard evidence that the above test message may have been intercepted by this unknown communicator was seen that on August 28, 1988, a strong and repeated message of the Greg Radio was received with the message finally terminated with the series SE (or 31).

"Further evidence that these may be actually communication attempts is seen in that on October 11, 1988... a very different approach was seen: A series of Greg Radio's was sent at about the normal code speed of about 5 words per minute, followed by KKTT, and then the series was repeated at a slower speed and also followed by KKTT.

"Another confirmation that these may be 'messages' appeared on October 12, 1988... Here, a series of A's and R's (with Greg Radio occasionally inserted) was then followed by Greg Radio sent as a series of five repetitions of each letter, e.g., Greg was sent as GGGGGGRRRRREEEEEGGGGG.

"Sufficient 'messages have now been received to indicate that perhaps a serious attempt to contact this writer was being made by some 'unknown communicator'. While this communicator may yet be some terrestrial experimenter, the possibility still exists that the communicator may be 'extraterrestrial' for the following reasons:

"A. The messages are in simple code (e.g., dits and dahs) type of pulses which would be expected to be used if one intelligent civilization were to try to contact another civilization in terms of pulses. That some of the simplest pulse signals are similar to simple Morse Code signals is more than coincidence — they are both based upon the same premises>

"B. Numbers are not in the complicated Morse Code symbols, but are in simple sequence, using short pulses or dits.

"C. The 'communicator' has recognized the coherent nature of Greg Radio and is possibly using that sequence of codes in various fashions to indicate that a 'contact' has been made.

"D. The communicator thus far has not responded to 'word' messages or the amateur Q-code signals. Thus it is believed that while some apparently Morse Code signals are being used, the communicator is not really familiar with such usage, other than recognizing the coherent nature of the signals.

"E. Since these messages at present appear largely near the noon hour, they may be coming from a definite source in space. At present, it is believed to be from the general direction of the constellation, Andromeda, but not necessarily the Galaxy there.

"There is also some possibility that this communicator may be 'extraterrestrial', perhaps yet in our solar system (Mars?), but no further than our own Galaxy or

Local Group of Galaxies. This same communicator may have been trying to reach here ever since the turn of the century when Nikola Tesla reported the interception of scalar S signals!"

In February, 1989, Hodowanec wrote this brief, untitled report: "Without going into the details of how this was determined: ET may be on Mars!

"This, in spite of NASA's denial of any life forms on Mars [which situation changed in 1996]. This possibility has been recently suspected by the writer due to the apparently very close tracking of my position on Earth by ET. ET, of course, always knew that I was on Earth (as seen by his tracking), but now he has most emphatically confirmed that he is on the 4th planet from the sun, i.e., Mars!

"While this release is probably a bit premature, I am so positive of these gravity signal 'exchanges' that I will stick my neck out in this instance. ET on Mars is apparently much more advanced than we are here on Earth, and he may have even previously visited here on Earth, and possibly colonized here (but who are his possible descendants?).

"It is still a mystery on where ET may be living on Mars (possibly underground near the polar regions?), and why ET doesn't use EM wave signaling methods?? Perhaps, it is because Mars is so hostile now that ET must have developed a very sophisticated underground civilization which is not conducive to EM radiation systems?

"This material is being released now confidentially to but a very few active colleagues until further confirmations on this assertion are obtained."

In his *Mars Flash* Number One (3/28/89) and Number Two (3/30/89), Hodowanec notified colleagues that, "As the result of the continued gravity signal communications between GH Labs and the Martians, the following extraordinary facts have come to light.

"The exchanges are now being made in terms of short 'English' code words for certain items. For example, the Martians now understand that FACE means the human face, MAN means the human person, Earth now means our planet, and Mars means their planet! They had originally tried some of their terminology with me, but gave up except where it made sense to me. For example, I now know that TTT at the end of their names means person and OOTTAEERR is their name for the 10th planet!"

In a handwritten footnote to the above article, Hodowanec informed Nelson that the Martian's name is "AAAAAATTT": "He appears to 'understand' my messages, even though I may have to repeat them in several ways so that he can 'see' the meaning.

"Communications between GH Labs and a Martian intelligence now continue with increasing progress since we have been able to establish over 50 simple expressions (most in simple English) for many of the common 'ideas' that we have. Martian AAAAAATTT is extremely adept in relating my English terminology to these common Earth-Mars observations.

"Mars has also confirmed that they are also 'men' with one 'head' that have two 'eyes' that 'see'. Also, they have one 'body' with two arms that have hands with five fingers each. Also they have two legs with two feet that have five toes each. I haven't been able to have them confirm the nose and mouth in the face, but that could be confirmed shortly, since those features appear in the FACE.

"Probably the most significant fact which was determined on this date seems to be that Mars is most emphatic that Earth men are like Mars men! This appears more and more that Mars has colonized Earth in the remote past! This could be true since we on Earth have never really found the 'missing link' between Earth humanoids and humans."

In a letter written in March, 1989 to Robert Nelson, Hodowanec states that "Generally, our contacts are limited to 20-30 minutes... since there appear to be other ETs out there interested in joining in also, and so there is some interference after a while. Some of these other ETs use other methods of communications such as tones and what appear to be guttural voices!

"ET is probably more advanced then we are on Earth. We no longer exchange simple arithmetic, and when I sent him Pi to five decimal places, he sent Pi back to seven decimal places immediately! We had discussed our nine planet solar system, but ET came back with ten planets, calling the 10th planet OOTTAEERR! When questioned on this, ET kept on confirming the existence of a tenth planet! He now knows the other nine planets by their Earth names! He also confirmed that Mars has two moons, the Earth one, and that Jupiter has nine major moons.

"These contacts are getting to be more interesting all the time, and ET appears to be most anxious to continue them. However, I just cannot spend too much time with him... I got across to him that I am just one person here communicating with him, and that the rest of Earth presently does not recognize the existence of any life on Mars.

"I have now had over 100 contacts with ET and can reach him at any time of day or night. We have also established some simple codes for acknowledgments and go ahead and respond. While we use these simple codes in many contexts, both ET and I now understand in which context they are being used!

"The Martians are apparently the advanced civilization, for they are the ones generating the 'modulated oscillated beam' which is now tracking my location on earth and is thus the means of our communications. [The beam is only about 15 miles in diameter here on Earth, but 1012 inches on Mars.]

"There is an apparent 'team' on Mars which is involved in these contacts. The original contact, ET Number One, with whom I have established the initial relationship, is apparently the most highly knowledgeable and advanced. The others who sometimes 'man' the Mars station appear to be less knowledgeable and some only request or acknowledge a transmission.

"Mars is most desperate to continue these contacts. The exchanges are made in many varied ways which cannot be readily predicted in order to convey the fact that these are real contacts

"Also, one can recognize the 'fist' of the one 'keying' these codes, e.g., ET Number One always sends clean letters or numbers, and identifies himself and me in some fashion. The other ETs on Mars usually don't. Therefore, no automation is being used here.

"While these contacts were originally due to a serendipitous circumstances, it is really the result if my gravitational communication experiments and thus a direct result from Rhysmonic Cosmology. And yet, however fantastic and unreal this may seem, it is real, and if also it is confirmed by one of you, it will be a major milestone in the history of mankind! Perhaps, if one of you finally 'hears' the modulations of 1/f noise background, you may try to establish your own contacts?"

Gregory Hodowanec has also had extreme reservations about the seriousness of the situation, which he expressed it in a letter dated April 4, 1989 to Nelson.

"...my 'contacts' with Mars continue with much information being exchanged. However, due to the increasingly astounding nature of these exchanges, I am now limiting further releases to only two long-time observers (witnesses) of my research efforts. This is being done so as not to jeopardize these contacts with unwanted notoriety or publicity in the media. There are now nine 'Mars Flashes' for the record. Perhaps, in the future, I may release some of these.

"...gravity signal communications are instantaneous, require extremely small energy expenditure, [unlike Tesla's experiments] and are so simple as to be just unbelievable by the average person. However, this is as far as I want to go with release of details at this time.

"I would appreciate that you keep this info somewhat confidential now. The Earth may not be ready for what I will have to say eventually. Nothing dire, just fantastic and thus perhaps unbelievable!"

## Could It Really Have Been Mars?

Even though critics of Tesla laughed at his belief that he may have received radio broadcasts from Mars, astronomers and other scientists of Tesla's day were openly speculating on the reality of intelligent life on Mars. So just how far-fetched is it to consider that someone was sending signals to Earth from Mars?

Tesla never gave up the idea of communicating with other worlds. In 1931, on the occasion of his 75th birthday interview for the cover story of *Time* magazine, he said the following: "I think that nothing can be more important than interplanetary communication. It will certainly come some day, and the certitude that there are other human beings in the universe, working, suffering, struggling, like ourselves, will produce a magic effect on mankind and will form the foundation of a universal brotherhood that will last as long as humanity itself."

Since early man first looked up to the heavens, Mars' ruddy glow has been an object of fascination for generations of star gazers. The Babylonians said the planet was Nergal, God of War. To the Greeks, Mars was their war god, Ares.

The Roman god, Mars assumed many of the characteristics and myths of Ares, and was the second-highest-ranking god in the Roman pantheon. Mars loved violence and battle.

According to Homer, even Jupiter, the father of Mars, recognized his son's bad attitude, saying to him, "Of all the gods of Olympus, I find you the most unpleasant and unlikable, for you enjoy nothing but violence, war and battles. You have a stubborn and mean disposition."

In excavations at Nineveh in northern Iraq, there was discovered in the library of King Assurbanipal clay cylinders on which is described a voyage to the sky. It narrates how King Eitan, who lived about 5,000 years ago, was taken as an honored guest on a flying ship in the shape of a shield which landed in a square behind the royal palace, rotating, surrounded by a vortex of flames. From the flying ship alighted tall, blond men with dark complexions dressed in white, handsome as gods, who invited King Eitan, to go for a trip.

In the middle of a whirlwind of flames, King Eitan went so high that the Earth with its seas, islands, continents, appeared to him as "a loaf in a basket." King Eitan in the flying ship reached Mars, Venus and the moon.

After two weeks absence, the flying ship glided over the city (Nineveh) and touched down surrounded by a ring of fire. King Eitan descended with some of the blond men who stayed as his guests for several days.

Of all the planets in the solar system besides Earth, Mars was thought to be the most likely to harbor intelligent life. Popular culture in the form of literature, radio and film, reflect such beliefs.

In 1659, Dutch astronomer Christiaan Huygens (1629-1695), used a telescope of his own design and drew the first sketch of Mars. Huygens also recorded the first true feature on Mars, a large dark spot, probably Syrtis Major.

Observing the spot in successive rotations, he deduced a 24 hour Martian day. In 1698, Huygens published COSMOTHEOROS, one of the earliest expositions on possible extraterrestrial life on the red planet. In this book, Huygens discusses what is required for a planet to be capable of supporting life and speculates about intelligent Martians.

Huygens' theories were ahead of his time as contemporary scientists loudly ridiculed the Dutch astronomer's work, calling into question his scientific integrity and past discoveries. It was not until years later that Huygens' early findings on Mars were confirmed by astronomers using more powerful and sophisticated telescopes.

The British Astronomer Frederick William Herschel (1738-1822), did various studies of Mars between 1777 and 1783 using small telescopes which he manufactured himself.

Herschel noted the seasonal changes of the polar caps and suggested they were made of snow and ice. He also speculated that vegetation may be growing during the Martian spring and summer. He wrongly considered that dark areas he had spotted to be oceans. Herschel believed that Mars was inhabited, he also felt there were intelligent beings living on all the planets, even in cool areas under the hot surface of the sun.

# The Lost Journals of Nikola Tesla

## Communicating With Mars

The April 13, 1892 edition of the newspaper *Spectator* carried an article entitled, *Telegraphing to Mars with solar signals*. This was one of the first articles that dealt with the language difficulties involved in communicating with the Martials, ( Martials was 19th century slang for Martians).

The article points out that mathematical information could be exchanged, but questions how we will communicate abstract concepts, such as "How are we to ask if Martials have engineers and ships, and electric lights and glaciers and five senses, and heads and feet?"

That same year, Nicloas Camille Flammarion published Volume one of his encyclopedia of *La Planète Mars*. Flammarion suggested the natural magnetism of the Earth might be harnessed to propagate sounds across space in order to communicate with life forms on Mars.

In 1877, Giovanni Schiaparelli observed and sketched what he referred to as Canali (Italian for channels) on the surface of Mars. Schiaparelli's drawings were remarkably extensive and soon drew worldwide attention.

In the early 1900's, Boston astronomer Percival Lowell corroborated and added to Schiaparelli's sketches, with his small telescope, Lowell took photographs of Mars that seemed to confirm the canals' existence.

Percival believed that Mars was covered with an intricate system of canals, not open water, but instead strips of vegetation along a subterranean irrigation system. The theory at the time was that the main water supply on Mars came from the polar ice caps. Seasonal melting would distribute water to the slowly dying planet through a grid of underground channels.

In 1954, when Mars made one of its close approaches to Earth, the National Geographic Society and Lowell Observatory arranged for the first worldwide "Mars Patrol." This effort, directed by Dr. Earl Slipher of the Lowell Observatory, attempted to gather better information and photographs of features on the surface of Mars.

The results once again seemed to show what appeared to be major canal lines across the surface of Mars, as well as evidence of vegetation that seemed to grow and then die back in connection to the Martian seasons. News of the photographs was leaked to astronomy journals such as *Sky & Telescope*, but the long-awaited public announcement of the "Mars Patrols" results never came.

# The Lost Journals of Nikola Tesla

## Life On Mars

In a pamphlet titled, *The Truth About Mars*, written in 1956, author Ernest L. Norman claimed to have contacted the inhabitants of planet Mars. In his booklet, Norman stated that he would spend an hour each evening in meditation, and that due to his meditations he was contacted in February of 1955 by a man from Mars.

"After introducing himself as Nur El, he quickly explained that he was from the planet Mars, and that if I so desired, I could go there with him, to his city (in astral flight) and that he would be my personal guide.

"He explained that his people were very desirous in view of all the controversy going on, to clear up some of the so-called mysteries of Mars. Our trip there is a matter of split seconds as no craft is used or needed.

"Arriving on the surface of Mars, we are at once aware of the extremely rugged terrain, rocky hills and sandy wastes, that stretches out endlessly around us. Nur El explains that the ionosphere is very thin which leaves the surface almost unprotected from the various beta, gamma and cosmic rays. This high concentration of rays ionizes the very rare and gaseous atmosphere and together with thermal currents, creates terrific dust storms.

"There is also a very thinly divided dust layer on the ionosphere which helps create the reddish appearance of the planet. There are also a number of volcanoes, three of which are of major size; one of these was just barely visible on the horizon trailing a thin wisp of smoke from its truncated cone.

"It was also explained that as Mars has only seven degrees axis inclination there is not much of a seasonal change. Water is very scarce on this arid planet; most of the precipitation falls at the poles. Vegetation is also scarce."

Norman continues his story saying, "On Mars the cities are all underground and are connected together by huge oval metal tubes from three to five hundred feet in diameter. It is these tubes which have confused the astronomers on the earth. Some believe them to be canals of either intelligent design, or using natural features to transport scarce water throughout the planet.

"The shifting desert sands often cover or uncover them which leads to further confusion inasmuch as they seem to appear and disappear. The people of Mars are smaller than those on earth, only averaging about four feet six inches in height.

"They are somewhat Mongolian in appearance. The Martians originally migrated in spacecraft to Mars from a dying planet more than a million years ago. They also came to this earth and started a colony but found it impractical to maintain. It was also explained by Nur El that this colony became our Chinese race through the evolution of time."

The Martians explained to Norman that more than 100,000 years ago Mars was much like Earth. There was air, water, and an abundance of plant and animal life.

At that time, through their occult science and also with their superior telescopes they saw, somewhere out in space, a cataclysm take place. A giant sun suddenly flared up like a nova and then exploded. Huge chunks hurtled out into space in different directions, each one a smaller, white-hot, "atomically-burning sun."

It was determined by calculations, that one of these fiery pieces would pass very close to our solar system. The Martians had a choice, to stay on Mars or to migrate to another planet far away from this solar system. After a search, it was found that there was no other planet available which would be suitable. So an alternative was decided upon. They could build huge cities underground.

After the cataclysm struck the solar system, Mars was left decimated and burnt. Earth as well suffered, there were great earthquakes and tidal waves as Earth's orbit and axis were changed drastically.

Ernest Norman's story, while similar to other esoteric writings of the time, is interesting because of his observations of climatic conditions on Mars that were not known by scientists in the 1950's. His statement concerning volcanoes on Mars was truly prophetic considering that at the time his booklet was written, Mars was not considered to have been seismically active.

With the advancement of modern rockets, Mars became one of the first planets to receive the attention of space probes sent from Earth. Mars, though, has not been an easy planet to reach.

In November of 1962, The Soviets launched a Mars probe, called Mars 1, which was to rendezvous with the planet in June of 1963. However, just ten weeks before the scheduled encounter, the Soviets lost contact with the spacecraft. Three years later the Soviets launched another probe called Zond 2, which was set to fly by Mars. This probe as well lost contact with Earth in April 1965.

In 1969, the United States sent the Mariner 7 probe to the red planet. In 1970 the probe lost radio communications with Earth, started tumbling out of control, its battery went dead, and the spacecraft 's velocity increased.

Mysteriously, a few hours later Mariner 7 suddenly ceased tumbling, radio communications were restored and the spacecraft's velocity returned to normal, despite the fact that its rocket system was inoperative. Nervous scientists began joking about "The Great Galactic Ghoul" lying in wait for unsuspecting spacecraft to fly by.

The term Great Galactic Ghoul was named by *Time* Magazine correspondent Donald Neff following the strange events surrounding the flight of Mariner 7. "The legend of the Great Galactic Ghoul is like the legend of the Bermuda Triangle," commented John Casani of the Jet Propulsion Laboratory.

The Soviets as well continued to lose Mars probes. On July 12, 1988 the USSR launched Phobos II, an unmanned satellite to Mars. It arrived in January 1989 and entered an orbit around Mars as the first phase towards it's real destination, the small Martian moon called Phobos.

The mission was flawless until the craft aligned itself with the moon. On March 28, 1989 an elliptical object was detected moving towards the satellite seconds before it lost communication with Earth. All indications were that the elliptical object had possibly attacked the satellite which was now dead and left spinning out of control.

On March 28, 1989, Tass, the official Soviet news agency stated: "Phobos II failed to communicate with Earth as scheduled after completing and operation yesterday around the Martian moon Phobos. Scientists at mission control have been unable to establish stable radio contact."

The next day a top official of the Soviet Space Agency (Glavkosmos) said: "Phobos II is 99% lost for good."

On March 31, 1989 headlines dispatched by the Moscow correspondents of the European News Agency (EFE) stated: "Phobos II Captured Strange Photos of Mars Before Losing Contact With It's Base. Vremya revealed yesterday that the space probe Phobos II, which was orbiting above Mars when Soviet scientists lost contact with it on Monday, had photographed an UNIDENTIFIED OBJECT on the Martian surface seconds before losing contact."

Scientists described the unidentified object as a thin ellipse 20 kilometers long. It was further stated that the photos could not be an illusion because it was captured by two different color cameras as well as cameras taking infrared shots.

One controller at the Kaliningrad control center concluded that the probe was now spinning out of control. It would seem that something struck or shot the

Phobos II Probe. In the October 19, 1989 issue of *Nature* magazine, Soviet scientists concluded that the craft could be spinning because it was impacted by some unknown object.

Recent attempts to reach Mars have also met with mysterious and frustrating failures. On September 23 1999, nine months of space flight to Mars ended in disaster when NASA's first interplanetary weather satellite was destroyed. It is thought that the Mars Climate Orbiter entered Mars' atmosphere at too steep an angle and broke up or burned in the atmosphere.

The 1,387 pound orbiter was believed to have come within 37 miles of Mars' surface. Project manager Richard Cook, of NASA's jet propulsion laboratory, said: "We believe the spacecraft came in at a lower altitude than we predicted."

Ten weeks later, in early December, the Mars Polar Lander and its two detachable probes, mysteriously disappeared after what was thought to be an almost flawless mission. The final communication from Mars Polar Lander prior to landing indicated it was on course and working fine.

The spacecraft turned its antenna away from Earth, 12 minutes before landing to orient itself for entry into the Martian atmosphere. Its last radio signals arrived at Earth 14 minutes later, at 3:03 p.m. ET.

The $165 million NASA probe was designed to slice through Mars' thin atmosphere at a 12.25-degree angle, the margin of error was just half a degree, separate from its heat shield, deploy a parachute and fire a dozen thrusters before setting down — all without radio contact with Earth.

After touching down, the lander was to have unfurled its solar panels and deployed its antenna, and a few minutes later, radioed a message back to Earth. Also silent were the two basketball-size Deep Space 2 microprobes that were riding along with the lander.

The microprobes were to slam into the planet at 400 mph as the main spacecraft descended, their fall unbroken by parachutes or thrusters. NASA controllers did not receive any signals from the two microprobes during the contact opportunities.

To this day, nothing was ever heard from the Polar Lander or its separate probes. While NASA was accused of covering up earlier reports that the Mars mission was doomed from the start due to human errors - the ultimate fate of the Polar Lander is shrouded in mystery.

It is almost as if someone or something is deliberately trying to stop our space probes from reaching Mars. This scenario on the surface seems absurd, but is it?

# The Lost Journals of Nikola Tesla

## Civilizations On Mars

In 1959 a Martian spacecraft reportedly landed in the wilderness outside of Moscow, in the Soviet Union, where a secret meeting with Soviet Premier Nikita Kruschev was arranged. The conference regarded improving relations with Earth, exchanging knowledge, and securing world and interplanetary peace, yet the Soviet government rejected the terms. This report originated from Sgt. Willard Wannall, formerly of Army Intelligence, who investigated UFOs in Hawaii while in the military in the 1950's.

On April 24, 1964, an oval shaped metallic flying object landed in a farm field in Newark Valley in New York State, and two alien beings emerged from the estimated 20 foot long craft. Farmer, Gary Wilcox drove his tractor toward the object clearly visible on a bright sunny day. The farmer kicked the metallic object to make sure it was real.

The two occupants were about four feet tall, and they carried a square tray full of the different vegetables they had collected from his farm. Wilcox reported that when he confronted the beings stealing his crops, they said: "Don't be alarmed, we have spoken to people before."

Gary described the voices as being very strange. They wore white, metallic-looking overalls without seams, stitching or pockets. He could not see their hands or feet. Nor could he see their faces beneath the full space-suits, which Wilcox speculated were protecting these aliens from the poisons in Earth's atmosphere.

As Wilcox became inquisitive, one of them stated: "We are from what you know as the planet Mars. We can only come to Earth every two years," and left a warning that Earth people should stay out of space. They said that they were studying the organic materials on Earth because of the rocky structure of Mars, and that they did not fly near our cities because they avoided the air pollution.

Wilcox gave the beings a bag of fertilizer and exchanged information about agriculture and mankind's attempts at spaceflight. Wilcox was later investigated by a psychiatrist and the sheriff department, who found him a normal, truthful person with no apparent emotional problems.

In February 1972, United Nations diplomat Farida Iskiovet, who investigated UFOs and occupant contacts for the President of the General Assembly, revealed that she had been contacted by a landed spacecraft from the planet Mars. The reported contact took place in the Mojave Desert, in California, in 1971, and made the front page" of the major Arizona newspaper the daily *Arizona Republic.*

This story also made the front page of the *San Clemente Sun-Post* in an article written by Fred Swegles. Farida stated that the alien offered to admit an ambassador to their interplanetary confederation in this solar system, in exchange for an alien ambassador to the General Assembly of the United Nations.

Allegedly, this was an attempt to re-establish diplomatic relations with Earth and other planets that had been suspended in ancient times due to hostility on Earth. However, the terms of this peace arrangement were not acceptable to the Security Council, and the exchange was allegedly rejected in a secret meeting.

Tesla may have been the first to hear strange radio transmissions from space, but he certainly was not the last. Some of the world's leading astronomers have revealed that they have collected more than 100 unexplained radio signals during routine surveillance of space.

These faint, pure tones have no natural origin and could have been created artificially, the scientists said. They do not rule out the astonishing possibility that this strange radio traffic could have extraterrestrial origins.

Most of the signals have been picked up by American radio telescopes managed by the Search for Extra-Terrestrial Intelligence Institute (SETI) in Mountain View, California, set up in 1988 to study radio static in space and scan it for material that could be evidence of alien contact. A few have also been logged by British astronomers studying stars and galaxies with the Lovell telescope at Jodrell Bank, near Macclesfield in Cheshire.

"It's tempting to hypothesize that at least some of these seductive signals were truly from ET and that they vanished from the ether when the extraterrestrials turned off their transmitters or otherwise went off air before we could verify the message," said Dr Seth Shostak, SETI's public programs scientist.

Alternatively, he said, it was possible they were simply the product of some kind of local interference that did not repeat when the astronomers tried to relocate the rogue signals.

SETI, which was formed by scientists including Carl Sagan and received funding from NASA until 1993, has reportedly yet to discover any clear, repeated radio pattern that might hint at the existence of alien intelligence in the universe. The short, indistinct signals are not considered good evidence of ET.

"If you could hear the signal at the frequency it is received, it would sound like a faint whistle, a pure tone which could only be made by a transmitter. As far as we know, nature can't make a pure sound," said Shostak. Each time one of these signals is detected by a radio telescope, an alarm alerts SETI astronomers, who work around the clock. None has yet been pinpointed or recorded a second time, so that scientists have been denied the chance of making a study of their source or composition.

"I'm sure there are signals that have come and gone that we couldn't get to the bottom of. That's not to say it's little green men trying to communicate with us, but we just don't know," said Dr Tom Muxlow, an astronomer at the British radio astronomy observatory. He disclosed that Jodrell Bank had picked up about six rogue signals.

The possibility that the signals have extra-terrestrial origins cannot be ignored, according to Nobel laureate Tony Hewish, emeritus professor of radio astronomy at Cambridge University. In 1967 Hewish and Jocelyn Bell, a student, believed they had found evidence of an alien first contact when they detected a regular pulse of radio signals coming from a distant star.

"It all had an air of unreality about it, but for a month we thought it was possible that the signals were coming from intelligent life on another planet. When radio astronomers pick up signals that are very peculiar they take it with a big pinch of salt, but you cannot remove the possibility," said Hewish. Instead, they had found a pulsar, a rapidly spinning neutron star, a discovery for which Hewish won a Nobel prize in 1974.

# The Lost Journals of Nikola Tesla

During experiments at Colorado Springs in 1899, Tesla began to receive radio signals of a highly unusual nature. He would later write: *"Although I could not at the time decipher their meaning, it was impossible for me to think of them as having been entirely accidental. The feeling is constantly growing on me that I had been the first to hear the greeting of one planet to another. A purpose was behind these electrical signals."*

# Chapter Four
## *Extraordinary Experiences*

Much has been made over Tesla's amazing ability to visualize images from his mind. This talent came mostly involuntarily and often at inopportune moments. When he was younger, Tesla worried that he was suffering from some sort of madness when his visions would appear. Later he came to realize that this particular trait was a gift and the basis of all his inventions.

Tesla's visions were so vivid that he was sometimes unsure of what was real and what imaginary. Strong flashes of light often accompanied these images. He would wave his hand in front of his eyes to determine whether the objects were simply in his mind or outside.

In 1919, Tesla wrote of these images and of his efforts to find an explanation for them. He had consulted with several doctors and psychologists, but no one was able to help.

"The theory I have formulated is that the images were the result of a reflex action from the brain on the retina under great excitation. They certainly were not hallucinations, for in other respects I was normal and composed.

"To give and idea of my distress, suppose that I had witnessed a funeral or some such nerve wracking spectacle. Then, inevitably, in the stillness of the night, a vivid picture of the scene would thrust itself before my eyes and persist despite all my efforts to banish it. Sometimes it would even remain fixed in space though I pushed my hand through it."

It is well known that Tesla's conception of his AC (alternating current) motor came to him during one of his visions. "One afternoon . . . I was enjoying a walk with my friend in the city park and reciting poetry. At that age I knew entire books by heart, word for word. One of these was Goethes Faust. The sun was just setting and reminded me of a glorious passage: *The glow retreats, done is the day of toil; It yonder hastes, new fields of life exploring; Ah, that no wing can lift me from the soil Upon its tract to follow, follow soaring!*

"As I uttered these inspiring words the idea came like a flash of lightning and in an instant the truth was revealed. I drew with a stick on the sand the diagram shown six years later in my address before the American institute of Electrical Engineers.

"The images were wonderfully sharp and clear and had the solidity of metal. 'See my motor here; watch me reverse it.'"

Tesla used his incredible power throughout his amazing career. He disliked drawing his conceptions down onto paper because they lacked the reality that Tesla's internal drawing board could provide. For Tesla, drawing was utterly unrealistic and a nuisance.

He did not have to make plans and jot down dimensions, because of this power of instant recall. He could store any designs in his mind to be retrieved intact years later.

Despite his unusual abilities, Tesla at first had little patience with those who believed in psychic powers or spirits. Tesla often denied that he had supernatural powers or origins from beyond the earth. Such allegations, along with his conviction in the reality of extraterrestrials, almost certainly hurt Tesla's reputation later in his life.

Tesla felt so strongly about such claims that he frequently wrote about his frustrations with people who wanted to believe that he was more than an ordinary human being.

"The by far greater number of human beings are never aware of what is passing around and within them and millions fall victims of disease and die prematurely just on this account. The commonest, everyday occurrences appear to them mysterious and inexplicable.

"One may feel a sudden wave of sadness and rack his brain for an explanation, when he might have noticed that it was caused by a cloud cutting off the rays of the sun. He may see the image of a friend dear to him under conditions which he construes as very peculiar, when only shortly before he has passed him in the street or seen his photograph somewhere.

"When he loses a collar button, he fusses and swears for an hour, being unable to visualize his previous actions and locate the object directly. Deficient observation is merely a form of ignorance and responsible for the many morbid notions and foolish ideas prevailing.

"There is not more than one out of every ten persons who does not believe in telepathy and other psychic manifestations, spiritualism and communion with the dead, and who would refuse to listen to willing or unwilling deceivers?

"Just to illustrate how deeply rooted this tendency has become even among the clear-headed American population, I may mention a comical incident. Shortly before the war, when the exhibition of my turbines in this city elicited widespread comment in the technical papers, I anticipated that there would be a scramble among manufacturers to get hold of the invention and I had particular designs on that man from Detroit (Ford) who has an uncanny faculty for accumulating millions.

"So confident was I, that he would turn up some day, that I declared this as certain to my secretary and assistants. Sure enough, one fine morning a body of engineers from the Ford Motor Company presented themselves with the request of discussing with me an important project.

"Didn't I tell you?, I remarked triumphantly to my employees, and one of them said, 'You are amazing, Mr. Tesla. Everything always comes out exactly as you predict.'

"As soon as these hard-headed men were seated, I of course, immediately began to extol the wonderful features of my turbine, when the spokesman interrupted me and said, 'We know all about this, but we are on a special errand. We have formed a psychological society for the investigation of psychic phenomena and we want you to join us in this undertaking.'

"I suppose these engineers never knew how near they came to being fired out of my office. Ever since I was told by some of the greatest men of the time, leaders in science whose names are immortal, that I am possessed of an unusual mind, I bent all my thinking faculties on the solution of great problems regardless of sacrifice.

"For many years I endeavored to solve the enigma of death, and watched eagerly for every kind of spiritual indication. But only once in the course of my existence have I had an experience which momentarily impressed me as supernatural.

"It was at the time of my mother's death. I had become completely exhausted by pain and long vigilance, and one night was carried to a building about two blocks from our home.

"As I lay helpless there, I thought that if my mother died while I was away from her bedside, she would surely give me a sign. Two or three months before, I was in London in company with my late friend, Sir William Crookes, when spiritualism was discussed and I was under the full sway of these thoughts.

"I might not have paid attention to other men, but was susceptible to his arguments as it was his epochal work on radiant matter, which I had read as a student, that made me embrace the electrical career. I reflected that the conditions for a look into the beyond were most favorable, for my mother was a woman of genius and particularly excelling in the powers of intuition.

"During the whole night every fibre in my brain was strained in expectancy, but nothing happened until early in the morning, when I fell in a sleep, or perhaps a swoon, and saw a cloud carrying angelic figures of marvelous beauty, one of whom gazed upon me lovingly and gradually assumed the features of my mother. "The appearance slowly floated across the room and vanished, and I was awakened by an indescribably sweet song of many voices. In that instant a certitude, which no words can express, came upon me that my mother had just died. And that was true.

"I was unable to understand the tremendous weight of the painful knowledge I received in advance, and wrote a letter to Sir William Crookes while still under the domination of these impressions and in poor bodily health.

"When I recovered, I sought for a long time the external cause of this strange manifestation and, to my great relief, I succeeded after many months of fruitless effort. I had seen the painting of a celebrated artist, representing allegorically one of the seasons in the form of a cloud with a group of angels which seemed to actually float in the air, and this had struck me forcefully.

"It was exactly the same that appeared in my dream, with the exception of my mother's likeness. The music came from the choir in the church nearby at the early mass of Easter morning, explaining everything satisfactorily in conformity with scientific facts."

As Tesla grew older, he became more interested in spirituality and mankind's place in the universe. Tesla had remarked once about inventing a machine that could project human thoughts onto a screen, much like a modern television. This idea would continue to be on his mind up until the time of his death.

Dale Alfrey remembers several notations concerning Tesla's ideas on the nature of the human spirit and whether it continues on after physical death. Tesla had been brought up in a religious environment – but he had become more "humanistic" in his attitudes and considered physical life to be no more than a "automation of nature."

"Tesla became more open to the idea that there is a spirit or soul that continues in another plane of existence after death," recalls Alfrey. "At one point Tesla chided Edison for stealing his idea on using a form of radio to contact the dead."

# The Lost Journals of Nikola Tesla

## Voices in the Aether

After his initial reception of enigmatic radio signals in 1899, Tesla worked for many years to perfect the receiving and transmitting equipment that was needed to better pick up and translate the possible alien broadcasts. At first the signals were nothing more than rhythmic sounds, almost a morse code type of transmission he reported.

Around 1918, Tesla started to receive what he considered to be voice transmissions, except the voices he was picking up were not human. Instead, Tesla wrote that – "The sounds I am listening to every night at first appear to be human voices conversing back and forth in a language I cannot understand. I find it difficult to imagine that I am actually hearing real voices from people not of this planet. There must be a more simple explanation that has so far eluded me."

In 1925 Tesla wrote that – "I am hearing more phrases in these transmissions that are definitely in English, French and German. If it were not for the fact that the frequencies I am monitoring are unusable for terrestrial radio stations, I would think that I am listening to people somewhere in the world talking to each other. This cannot be the case as these signals are coming from points in the sky above the Earth."

Nikola Tesla may have been one of the first to receive strange radio signals that he thought were from beyond Earth, but he certainly wasn't the last. It is now known in the journals of Fortean that mysterious messages claiming extraterrestrial origins are being received repeatedly by ordinary, household electronics. Startled witnesses have reported strange signals emanating from turned off televisions and radios, as well as weird phone calls filled with electronic sounds and whispering voices.

In the early days of radio experimentation, hobbyists were amazed when their primitive sets would suddenly burst forth with strong, clear signals, far more powerful then any existing station at the time. The signals have often been explained away as normal radio interference caused by the weather or other natural sources.

In 1965, Soviet scientists Gennady B. Sholomitsky, Nikolai Kardashev and I. S. Shklovskii, received world wide attention when they announced that they had received radio signals from beacons of some super-civilization in space. These signals, they said, were ordered and indicative of interplanetary intelligence.

Later, other radio astronomers discovered that these signals were coming from celestial bodies that we now know as quasars. Other strange radio signals have not been as easily explained.

Dr. Hugh Mansfield Robinson, conducting a set of radio experiments in 1921, received intelligent signals on the thirty-thousand-meter wavelength. Ernest B. Rogers, the engineer in charge of the test felt compelled to state that "the signals were of extraterrestrial origin, as there were no sending instruments of that power on Earth at that time."

An amateur radio astronomer named Grote Reber reported receiving strong dot-and-dash signals from space in 1939. He had build a thirty-foot dish antenna in Wheaton, Illinois and said he often listened to the signals for eight hours at a time. They seemed to come from one specific spot in the sky. None of these early, mysterious signals have ever been explained.

## Long Delayed Echoes

Radio enthusiasts in the 1920s discovered a phenomenon which they labeled LDE (Long Delayed Echoes). Signals sent out from earth sometimes came bouncing back several seconds later, as if they had been reflected back by something in space. In a few instances some LDEs returned days, months, even years later. Researchers in Europe reported LDE's in 1927, 1928 and 1934. The echo pulses were delayed from three to fifteen seconds.

Dr. Ronald N. Bracewell of Stanford University speculated in 1962 that an alien satellite equipped with a computer which would scan all radio frequencies as it traveled through space, could be responsible for the strange LDEs. The satellite would pick up intelligent signals, record them and then rebroadcast it back on the same frequency.

Suppose, he thought, that the satellite was programmed so that if the message was returned again, indicating the system was understood, it would then transmit a message of its own. The LDEs of the 1920s could have come from such a satellite suggested Bracewell.

In the weekly scientific journal *Nature*, there appears in the issue of November 3, 1928, a letter written by one Jorgen Hals, a radio engineer of Bygodo, Oslo, to physicist Carl Stormer.

# The Lost Journals of Nikola Tesla

"At the end of the summer of 1927 I repeatedly heard signals from the Dutch short-wave transmitting station PCJJ at Eindhoven. At the same time as I heard these I also heard echoes. I heard the usual echo which goes round the Earth with an interval of about 1/7th of a second as well as a weaker echo about three seconds after the principal echo had gone.

"When the principal signal was especially strong, I suppose the amplitude for the last echo three seconds later, lay between 1/10 and 1/20 of the principal signal in strength. From where this echo comes I cannot say for the present, I can only confirm that I really heard it."

Stormer initiated certain tests as a result of this communication and on October 11, 1928, these achieved some success. During the afternoon of that day Station PCJJ in Eindhoven emitted very strong signals on 31.4 meters.

Both Hals and Stormer heard very distinct echoes several times, the interval between signal and echo varying between three and five seconds, most of them coming back about eight seconds after the principal signal. Sometimes two echoes were heard with an interval of about four seconds.

Physicist Van der Pol confirmed these observations in a telegram that read: "Last night special emission gave echoes here varying between three and 15 seconds. 50% of echoes heard after eight seconds!"

At the time these peculiarly long echoes were attributed by Stormer to auroral causes but the feeling today is that they have never been adequately explained. Six years later, in 1934, radio echoes of a similar kind from Holland were also heard.

A young Scottish astronomer named Duncan Lunan reviewed the LDE records of the 1920s and set out to decode them. He laid out the LDE data on a graph, using dots to represent the pauses between echoes. To his astonishment, a map began to take shape.

"The dots made up a map of an easily-recognized constellation," Lunan said. "The Constellation of Bootis in the northern sky. The curious pattern of delayed echoes was actually a pattern of star positions." Lunan worked up other LDE maps and found that they all seemed to center around Epsilon Bootis, a star in the constellation.

Lunan speculated that the LDEs were indicating that the point of origin for the alien satellite was the star system Epsilon Bootis. Lunan submitted his findings to the British Interplanetary Society. Kenneth Gatland, vice president of the society was enthusiastic about Lunan's findings.

"Lunan's findings are utterly astounding. I have studied the maps and must come to the same conclusions he did."

Unusual radio broadcasts are often reported in areas of high UFO activity. In January, 1954, people throughout the Midwest heard a voice coming through turned-off radios.

The voice, speaking in a dull monotone, stated: "I wish no one to be afraid, although I speak from space. But if you do not stop your preparations for war, you will be destroyed." This type of unusual broadcast has been heard by startled listeners worldwide. No earthly hoaxer was ever been caught or confessed.

On August 3, 1958, radio ham operators throughout the United States reportedly picked up a strange broadcast on the seventy-five-meter international band. A male voice claiming to be "Nacoma from the planet Jupiter" warned his listeners that the atomic bomb tests could lead to disaster. The voice spoke for two-and-a-half hours in English, German, Norwegian and his own language, described as a kind of musical gibberish.

"It was the most powerful signal ever picked up," one account said. "There was plenty of time during the broadcast for hundreds to listen, and radio operators called in friends and neighbors and phoned long distance to relatives in other states to listen in."

Author John Keel wrote in the September, 1977 issue of *UFO Report* that while in West Virginia, he visited a radio hobbyist and listened to strange sounds on a homemade VLF (Very Low Frequency) radio set.

"Strange voices were chattering back and forth on frequencies that supposedly cannot carry voice transmission. They spoke in a rapid-fire guttural language we could not identify. At first I thought it might be ordinary people speaking through a 'scrambler.' but later I sought out and listened to samples of voice transmissions through different kinds of scramblers and there was no similarity."

According to the Spanish newspaper *El Diario De Nueva York*, on January 31, 1950, UFO activity over Madrid, Spain was accompanied by unusual radio broadcasts.

"In the last two days, near midnight, intense phosphorescence and the forms of strange lights have been observed at the same time. They have passed through the sky from north to south, and radio receivers have heard, during the occurrence of this phenomenon, words pronounced in an incomprehensible tongue. Popular fancy supposes that these luminous signals may come from the planet Mars."

# The Lost Journals of Nikola Tesla

Strange voices speaking a guttural, unknown language has been often associated with inexplicable radio broadcasts. Nor has this phenomena been contained to anecdotal tales from untrained individuals. Since its inception, NASA has experienced unauthorized radio interference problems of one form or another on practically every manned space mission.

A good example was the Mercury Faith 7 flight with Astronaut Gordon Cooper. On May 15, 1963, during his forth pass over Hawaii, Cooper's voice transmission was suddenly interrupted and drowned out by "an unintelligible foreign language transmission" on the channel reserved for space flights - a frequency which few if any amateurs were equipped to broadcast on.

If the signal came from the ground, it had to come from Hawaii, but the FCC never solved the mystery. NASA recorded the transmission, which sounded like a voice grunting and speaking rapidly in a language that has never been identified.

## The Search For Extraterrestrial Intelligence

In 1955 two Cornell University physicists, Giuseppi Cocconi and Philip Morrison, published a paper suggesting it might be possible to use microwave radio to communicate between the stars. By pointing a radio telescope at a near by, Sun-like star that might have planets, astronomers might be able to detect radio waves generated by intelligent life there. Since 1960, The Search for Extra-terrestrial Intelligence (SETI) has been carried on by scientific researchers.

Radio waves are considered the best means available, given current technology, for trying to detect extra-terrestrial intelligence. Radio waves travel at the speed of light (which is the fastest theoretical speed possible) which is about 300,000 kilometers a second.

At this speed a signal sent from our nearest neighbor star, Proxima Centauri, takes over four years to reach Earth. This may seem like a long time, but the fastest space probe currently built would take 300,000 years to make the same trip.

Radio astronomer Frank Drake was the first to attempt a SETI search by using an 85 foot antenna at Greenbank, West Virginia, to listen in the direction of two nearby stars, Tau Ceti and Epsilon Eridani.

For two months he monitored the stars for signals at 1,420 MHz, a frequency associated with hydrogen, which was chosen as a logical channel to listen to because of its astronomical significance (Hydrogen is the most abundant element in the Universe). Unfortunately, Drakes project achieved no positive results.

Additional SETI programs were conducted in the Soviet Union through the 1960's but the next serious attempt in the United States wasn't made until the early 70's when NASA's Ames Research Center put together a team of experts to consider how an effective search could be done.

The result was known as Project Cyclops. Radio astronomers, using the work in the Cyclops report, started conducting searches throughout the 70's using existing antennas and receivers.

## The "WOW!" Signal

In 1977 Dr. Jerry Ehman was involved in a search for signals of an artificial origin using the "Big Ear" antenna (now replaced by a golf course) at Ohio State University. Out of this effort came one of the most interesting, and mystifying, signals to date. Known as the "Wow!" signal (after the exclamation written by Dr. Ehman next to a particularly tantalizing part of the computer printout), it still remains unexplained.

The "Wow!" source radio emission entered the receiver of the Big Ear radio telescope at about 11:16 p.m. Eastern Daylight Savings Time on August 15, 1977. Dr. Ehman had worked at OSU as an assistant professor in electrical engineering and astronomy. When the National Science Foundation cut funding to the Big Ear in 1972, Dr. Ehman was let go, but he stayed on as a volunteer.

"A few days after the August 15, 1977 detection, I began my routine review of the computer printout from the multi-day run that began on August 15th. Several pages into the computer printout I was astonished to see the string of numbers and characters '6EQUJ5' in channel 2 of the printout.

"I immediately recognized this as the pattern we would expect to see from a narrowband radio source of small angular diameter in the sky. In the red pen I was using I immediately circled those six characters and wrote the notation 'Wow!' in the left margin of the computer printout opposite them.

"After I completed the review of the rest of the printout, I contacted Bob Dixon and Dr. John D. Kraus, the Director of the Big Ear Radio Observatory. They were astonished too. Then we began an analysis of what has been called for more then 20 years the "Wow! source.""

Could the signal actually be of extraterrestrial origin? Ohio State University researchers weren't sure. They trained the massive scope on that part of the sky for the next month, but the signal was never recorded again.

Dr. Ehman, who has continued his research on the "Wow!" signal, writes that after more than twenty years, the signal still remains a mystery.

"Even if it were intelligent beings sending a signal, they'd do it far more than once," Ehman says. "We should have seen it when we looked for it again. At this point we have eliminated any terrestrial sources for the signal. Thus, since all of the possibilities of a terrestrial origin have been either ruled out or seem improbable, and since the possibility of an extraterrestrial origin has not been able to be ruled out, I must conclude that an ETI (Extraterrestrial Intelligence) might have sent the signal that we received as the "Wow!" source.

"Of course, being a scientist, I await the reception of additional signals like the "Wow!" source that are able to be received and analyzed by many observatories. Thus, I must state that the origin of the "Wow!" signal is still an open question for me. There is simply too little data to draw many conclusions. In other words, I choose not to draw vast conclusions from 'half-vast' data."

Curious signals were picked up from 12 stars by the 300-foot radio telescope at Green Bank, WV, according to an article published in the January 29, 1978 edition of *The Baltimore Sun*. The signals took the form of strong bursts at a wavelength of 21 cm, one of the wave lengths characteristic of the hydrogen molecule.

Unfortunately, the signals were so short that their information content, if any, could not be recorded. Since the bursts were not repeated (except for a second burst from Barnard's Star), some natural phenomenon may be at work rather than intelligent communicators, who would presumably be more persistent.

The peculiar signals, which had never been recorded before, were discovered as part of Project Ozma II, in which radio astronomers listened to 21-cm radio waves from hundreds of nearby stars.

SETI is stepping up efforts to increase its chances of relocating one of these signals and has secured the use of the world's largest radio telescope at Arecibo in Puerto Rico. Scientists worldwide are excited by possible future discoveries.

SETI scientists are also negotiating with British astronomers to launch a five-year project to allow speedy verification and tracking of these elusive noises. Whenever SETI identifies a suspect signal, radio telescopes at Jodrell Bank will scan the same section of the sky to locate it. In this way the scientists can rule out possible terrestrial interference from radar, airplanes, even microwave ovens as a cause.

"I'm sure there are signals that have come and gone that we couldn't get to the bottom of. That's not to say it's little green men trying to communicate with us, but we just don't know," said Dr Tom Muxlow, an astronomer at the British radio astronomy observatory. He disclosed that Jodrell Bank had picked up about six rogue signals.

The possibility that the signals have extra-terrestrial origins cannot be ignored, according to Nobel laureate Tony Hewish, emeritus professor of radio astronomy at Cambridge University. In 1967 Hewish and Jocelyn Bell, a student, believed they had found evidence of an alien first contact when they detected a regular pulse of radio signals coming from a distant star.

"It all had an air of unreality about it, but for a month we thought it was possible that the signals were coming from intelligent life on another planet. When radio astronomers pick up signals that are very peculiar they take it with a big pinch of salt, but you cannot remove the possibility," said Hewish. Instead, they had found a pulsar, a rapidly spinning neutron star, a discovery for which Hewish won a Nobel prize in 1974.

Shostak is not put off by the prospect that any signal from an alien world would probably be indecipherable. "If we heard from an ET , it would be from a civilization that is a long way ahead of us, maybe even a million years more advanced than we are," he said.

Recently, Peter Backus, of Project Phoenix in California, believed that he was listening to messages from outer space via the 64-meter Parkes radio telescope in Australia. The telescope, the biggest in the southern hemisphere, picked up a distinct, but inexplicable, radio signal around 2.4 gigahertz at about the same time each evening.

However, a thorough investigation revealed that the scientists were not listening to other planets communicating through space. Instead, they were eavesdropping on meals cooking in the microwave oven downstairs.

"It was pretty loud," Dr. Backus told the annual meeting of the American Astronomical Society in San Antonio. "One time I tracked one signal for two hours. I couldn't rule it out as human noise. I was just about to tell my colleagues when I realized that the signal was suspiciously linked to break times."

# Chapter Five
*Tesla and Electronic Voice Phenomena*

No one can deny that computers and electronics have forever changed our way of life. There are electronic controls and computer chips in everything from the small appliances that toast our bread to the cars we drive, and make possible myriad forms of new entertainment, from VCRs and DVDs to video games and talking stuffed toys.

For a number of years some people have claimed that electronics can be useful in a quite unexpected way: to contact the dead, or at least allow the dead to contact us. Obviously, these claims are highly controversial. They make many assumptions: that there is life after death, that the dead are interested in contacting us, and that they have the means by which to do so.

The mysterious signals that Tesla received could be linked to what is now known as Electronic Voice Phenomena (EVP). Tesla was one of the first men to experiment with the necessary electronic receiving equipment. The very same equipment, albeit more sophisticated than Tesla had access to, is being used today to receive EVP.

Many people experimenting with Electronic Voice Phenomena (EVP) and Instrumental Transcommunication (ITC) say they have received messages from "the other side" through radios, tape recorders, VCRs, televisions, telephones, and even computers.

These phenomena have manifest themselves since the appearance of the instruments themselves. EVP, for example, has been reported for well over 50 years or more: Strange voices being picked up with primitive radios during WWI and heard faintly on magnetic recording tape.

Tesla may have been the first to receive these electronic voices from another plane of reality. As with other modes of communications with alleged discarnate entities, care must be taken not to be swayed by the stories often told by beings from the other side. Tesla may have been duped, so-to-speak, by voices that only pretended to be creatures from other planets.

This is nothing new to those who are familiar with the tall tales told to them by spirits who claim to be ascended masters, Abraham Lincoln or Ashtar of the Interplanetary Space Command. Spirits love to tell lies to anyone who will listen.

Those such as Tesla and Marconi who experimented with radio early on were the first to report anomalous sounds and voices emanating from their radio receivers. These early reports were looked upon as mildly interesting curiosities and quickly forgotten.

Theosophist Alice Bailey in 1936, transcribed these words of her great teacher, the Tibetan Master DK: "Within the next few years the fact of the eternity of existence will have advanced from the realm of questioning into the realm of certainty. Through the use of the radio by those who have passed over, will communication be set up and reduced to a true science."

It has been widely written that Edison and his assistant, Dr. Miller Hutchinson, were seriously at work building a machine to achieve spirit communication. Tesla wrote in his journals that Thomas Edison had heard from other engineers that Tesla had been receiving mysterious voices and sounds over radio frequencies that were not conducive for the broadcasting of the human voice.

Edison, who publically mocked Tesla and his experiments, privately believed that Tesla had managed to find the correct frequency to enable communication with spirits of the dead. Edison was determined to discover Tesla's secret, and be the first to get the "Spirit Phone" on the market.

In his diary, Dr. Miller Hutchinson wrote: "Edison and I are convinced that in the fields of psychic research will yet be discovered facts that will prove of greater significance to the thinking of the human race than all the inventions we have ever made in the field of electricity."

Edison failed to live long enough to succeed with his ill-gotten idea to best Tesla. Tesla simply noted in his journal that Edison was trying to use his patents to talk with specters. Edison thought that Tesla could listen to spirits, Tesla considered that he was hearing people from other planets – the voices could have been the same, they may have just changed their stories to fit the belief system of the listener.

In 1967, Edison allegedly spoke through West German clairvoyant Sigrun Seuterman, in trance, about his earlier efforts to develop equipment for recording voices from the beyond. Edison also made suggestions as to how to modify TV sets and tune them to 740 megahertz to get paranormal effects. (Session recorded on tape by Paul Affolter, Liestal, Switzerland).

On September 15, 1952, two Catholic priests, Father Ernetti and Father Gemilli were collaborating on a musical research project; Ernetti as an internationally respected scientist, physicist, philosopher and music lover, and Gemilli as President of the Papal Academy.

The two men were trying to record a Gregorian chant, but a wire in their equipment kept breaking. Exasperated, Gemilli looked up and asked his dead father for help. To his amazement his fathers voice was heard saying: "Of course I shall help you. I'm always with you." They repeated the experiment, and the voice, even clearer than before, said: "But Zucchini, it is clear, don't you know it is I?."

Gemilli was astonished. No one knew his childhood nickname but his father. The priest was suddenly afraid, for as a Catholic priest he had no right to speak with the dead. Troubled, the two men eventually sought an audience with Pope Pius XII in Rome.

Gemilli told the Pontiff of his experience, and to his surprise, was reassured. According to the 1990 translated text of his meeting, Pope Pius told Gemilli: "You really need not worry about this. The existence of this voice is strictly a scientific fact and has nothing whatsoever to do with spiritism. The recorder is totally objective. It receives and records sound waves from wherever they come. This experiment may perhaps become the cornerstone for a building for scientific studies which will strengthen people's faith in a hereafter."

Electronic Voice Phenomena was next researched by two men from California, the medium Attila von Szalay and paranormal researcher Raymond Bayless. In 1956, they recorded, quite by chance, a series of paranormal voices on magnetic tape, voices that should not logically have been there.

Though Bayless reported their experiments in the *Journal of the American Society for Psychical Research*, like Tesla years before, not a single person contacted the society or the researchers to enquire about their work.

It was not until 1959 when Friedrich Juergenson, a film producer in Sweden, first made public his amazing voice recordings, did the world sit up and take notice of the Tesla voice phenomena.

Juergenson, while making a documentary, had decided to try and tape bird songs. When he played the tape back he was startled to hear, in among the tweeting and chirping, what sounded like his mother's voice say in German: "Friedrich, you are being watched. Friedel, my little Friedel, can you hear me?"

Years later, Juergenson said that when he heard his mother's voice he was convinced he had made "an important discovery."

# The Lost Journals of Nikola Tesla

## Radio Contact With the Dead?

In 1967, Juergenson's *Radio Contact with the Dead* was translated into German, and Latvian psychologist Dr. Konstantin Raudive read it skeptically. He visited Juergenson to learn his methodology, decided to experiment on his own, and soon began developing his own experimental techniques.

Like Juergenson, Raudive too heard the voice of his own deceased mother, who called him by his boyhood name: "Kostulit, this is your mother." Eventually he catalogued tens of thousands of voices, many under strict laboratory conditions.

He published his book, *Unhoerbares Wird Hoerbar* (The Inaudible Becomes Audible), based on 72,000 voices he recorded.

In 1971, the chief engineers of Pye Records Ltd. decided to do a controlled experiment with Raudive. They invited him to their sound lab and installed special equipment to block out any radio and television signals. They would not allow Raudive to touch any of the equipment.

Raudive used one tape recorder which was monitored by a control tape recorder. All he could do was speak into a microphone. They taped Raudive's voice for eighteen minutes and none of the experimenters heard any other sounds. But when the scientists played back the tape, to their amazement, they heard over two hundred voices recorded on tape.

In the same year, Colin Smythe, Ltd. England, published expanded English translations of Raudive's book: *Breakthrough, an Amazing Experiment in Electronic Communication with the Dead.* Dr. Konstantin Raudive was a Latvian psychologist who had read Juergenson's book, *Radio Contact with the Dead*, with a great deal of scepticism when it was translated into German in 1967. Nevertheless he was intrigued and over several years carried out hundreds of experiments under laboratory conditions.

In the years that followed, Juergenson and Raudive continued their research that inspired countless others to emulate their experiments. But constant criticism that the EVP was nothing more than ambient sounds processed by the mind into a semblance of speech, or snatches of shortwave radio, dampened enthusiasm for research in Europe.

However, during the 1970s and early 80s in the United States, EVP continued to evolve with much of the work spearheaded by a retired engineer, George Meek. In 1971, Meek opened a small laboratory Philadelphia after a lifetime's interest in the paranormal. Meek soon became immersed in EVP – and realized its limitations. Meek was convinced that for electronic communication with the dead to really make its mark, apparatus more sophisticated than cassette recorders and AM radios would be necessary.

Meek decided that the best way to succeed was to attempt contact with someone who had passed on and work with him and his team in achieving two-way communication with the Other Side. The problem of course was gaining the initial contact.

Meek wrote to the now defunct American magazine *The Psychic Observer*, which put him in touch with Bill O'Neil, an electronics engineer who was also a gifted clairvoyant. Through O'Neil, Meek's team, later to form themselves into the Metascience Foundation, made contact with a man who claimed to have been dead for five years and who was a medical doctor while on earth.

"Doc Nick," as the discarnate became known, suggested to O'Neil that the team use certain audio frequencies instead of the white noise traditionally used by EVP researchers. This, he said, would serve as an energy source against which the sounds produced by his vocal cords could be played. The resulting experiments worked better than anyone had ever expected.

Soon after, a spirit being calling himself Dr. George Jeffries Mueller, was recruited to the team, or rather he announced he had come to join them after materializing one afternoon in O'Neil's living room. Mueller claimed to be a deceased university professor and NASA scientist.

Mueller told Meek and O'Neil that he had died in 1967 and gave them numerous facts with which to verify his identity including his security number; the place where his death certificate could be found; and intimate details of his life and scholastic achievements. All of them checked out.

He began communicating regularly; helping to design a new piece of electromagnetic equipment that would convert spirit voices to audible voices. On October 27, 1977, his first words were recorded on the new system Meek called Spiricom.

Tapes of the Mueller conversations were subsequently released to the public. The voice of Mueller can be plainly heard joking with Meek and O'Neil and discussing topics from his favorite foods to the view of time from the spirit world.

He gave unlisted telephone numbers asking them to make calls to confirm the identity (which they did successfully) of the people at the other end (usually top-level government personnel); and he gives O'Neil precise directions with which to help build experimental video equipment to take spirit communication to the next level.

The clarity of the communications is astounding – and sometimes amusing: in one conversation, Mueller identifies a problem with a particular device and impatiently barks at O'Neil: "The fault lies in an impedance mis-match which can be corrected by using a 150 ohm half-watt resistor in parallel with a 0.0047 microfad ceramic capacitor."

Eventually, Mueller ceased contact after telling Meek and O'Neil that natural law meant he could "not be here forever." (He did in fact return once more to a group of ITC researchers working in Rivenick, Germany, led by Adolph Homes. In 1991 they received on a TV screen an image which was said to be that of Dr Mueller).

Meek concluded that Mueller had progressed to a higher state of being to such a point that Spiricom could no longer be used for communication. Apparently, only beings closest to the Earth plane of existence, could communicate through the relatively primitive electronics.

It had become clear that the most limiting aspect of the device was the fact that it depended almost entirely on the operator possessing mediumistic or psychic abilities. Obviously, gifted individuals like Bill O'Neil, Dr. Konstantin Raudive and Nikola Tesla were a necessary component in the reception of signals and voices from the Aether.

Much like batteries energize a portable CD player, the vibrant field of energy that surrounds special people activates electronic equipment tuned to receive other realities. Without these people, it is doubtful that enough energy can be provided by the discarnate entity to achieve communication.

George Meek fully accepted this and never patented Spiricom. His hope was that science would carry on his work and take it to the next level, going beyond what he and O'Neil were able and unable to accomplish.

In 1982 Meek held a press conference in Washington, DC and revealed Spiricom's secrets. The conference made little impact on a largely skeptical world; in fact a large section of the media even refused to attend, so the device went largely unreported - except by the tabloids who naturally poked fun at the sensational story. Since that time, the focus of attention in terms of results has switched to Europe.

# The Lost Journals of Nikola Tesla

Nine months after Meek went public, on January 15, 1982, an electronics engineer named Hans-Otto Koenig, helped the now defunct Radio Luxembourg do a live broadcast on what was claimed to be a two-way conversation with a dead person.

Koenig had invented an ultrasound device after closely following Meek's work which, he claimed, could replicate the Spiricom and Mueller/O'Neil dialogues. The equipment was set up under the watchful eye of the Radio Luxembourg engineers.

The device, nicknamed *Koenig's Generator* by Rainer Holbe, the programs host, was connected to a set of speakers and switched on. An engineer asked over the air if any spirits cared to speak. Within seconds, a clear voice was heard. It said quite simply: "Otto Koenig makes wireless with the dead." Understandably pandemonium broke out in the studio.

Another question was asked and seconds later a voice replied: "We hear your voice." Rainer Holbe affirmed live on air there had been no trickery and later the station issued a statement stating that its engineers had found no natural explanation for what had happened.

Soon after, the device was demonstrated to members of the German EVP Association in Frankfurt where Konstantin Raudive, who had died in 1974, confirmed his presence. On the strength of this, one of Koenig's associates Dr Ernst Senkowski, a physics lecturer, electronics expert and veteran EVP researcher, persuaded George Meek to fly to Germany.

After a demonstration of the Koenig's Generator, Meek flew back convinced it was genuine and set about raising money to fund future work. Further research has been carried on by others in the field of electronics and radio who also have an interest in contacts with spirits.

Experiments held at a mansion in Newport Rhode Island have yielded some interesting results involving paranormal activity and the use of Shortwave Radio as a possible means of communication with other realities.

A research team led by Steve Cerilli has determined that tube based short-wave radios can provide a communication link with other planes of existence and their inhabitants. Recordings made on October 3, 1999 demonstrate that spirit entities can manipulate shortwave radios.

Curiously, the spirits present on that night learned how to better interact with the shortwave as the session progressed. By the end of the experiment, the entire room was awash with a form of static/electromagnetic energy. The tapes of this experiment are still undeveloped at this time.

Development of a paranormal recording involves re-dubbing the tape i.e. making multiple generations for reasons unknown. Research will be hopefully completed by the end of the decade.

A series of questions scripted by the research team were read by the owner of the location, which is known for its paranormal activity. The spirits were addressed and asked to participate in the experiment. The method of recording and equipment being used was then described. The questions asked were Socratic in nature, which means that they lead the listener to a revelation, each question building upon the former.

As a result of these experiments, all paranormal activity in the castle has stopped. It was the intention of the researchers to help these entities by achieving contact. The researchers felt that the spirits were somehow trapped or lost in between dimensions.

One possible scenario for disturbed spirit presences and haunting's is that due to a tragic event in an individuals lifetime, the desire to remain on this plane of time creates a state of suspension. Spirits in this suspended state become prisoners of their own inability to let go.

It is believe that by establishing a communication link with the shortwave and asking relevant questions (Socratic method), lost spirits can be freed from their suspended state and made aware that there is nothing outside their own consciousness holding them back.

One of the participants, Jennipher Roos, described her experience that night. "After spending the time it took to set up the equipment in the ballroom – about an hour, I walked outside to clear my thoughts and energy centers.

"Upon returning to the room, I could immediately feel changing vibrations with myself. I walked around the perimeter of the room in attempt to familiarize myself with my surroundings. I noticed a particularly strong feeling – highly sensational – in the corner of the room leading into the master bedroom.

"The only color of light I noticed before the experiments began, was a slight brightness in that corner of no particular color. The light surrounding the people participating in the study was nothing worth noting nothing out of the ordinary.

"During the first session, recording only, I was not aware of any overwhelming presence or energy disturbances. I was sitting on the floor – to the left of the

Mayan sculpture. I felt centered and secure at all times; and although the room was highly charged, I cannot report any great shifts in the overall energy of the space and no specific concentrations of electromagnetism. The only notable change I observed was that the light in the corner of the room by the master bedroom had increased in intensity and now had a slightly bluish tinge.

"The next session, which involved the short wave radio was quite an experience for me personally. I had moved to the corner of the room which I previously described as highly active.

"Once I was centered on the floor and the questions began I could immediately sense a presence of some kind. A slight vibration moved from the floor, through my bottom and thighs, up my spine and into my head. This sensation was exceptionally strong and caused all of my hairs to stand on end.

"I placed my hands palm down on the floor in front of me and received the same sensation through my hands and arms, which heightened incredibly the overall effect. I could see luminous light all around me and when I moved my hand in front of me, the light attached itself to me and left a streak of light, like a tracer, in its path of movement.

"The short-wave radio was definitely receiving some sort of transmission amongst the white noise, but it was very faint deviations to me. However, about half-way through this session I began to hear other noises in the room.

"The best way I can describe them is like a low tone of church bells played very slowly...almost like a drone, but in a pattern that was repeatedly louder at the beginning of each "chime." This sound was moving throughout the room in a circular fashion, like in stereo surround.

"As I focused all of my concentration and energy on the light and this sound, the short wave seemed to become more effected and I could definitely feel an increase of electromagnetic energy as the session progressed. At one point I was fairly overwhelmed with the feeling of it all...my body hair was on end for the entire session.

"I never observed any other colors at this time, nor did I feel that any of the participants, including myself were in any sort of danger. This part of the experiment was definitely the most powerful for me.

"I moved to the floor between the two aforementioned chairs and it was at this time that I started to notice huge changes in the short wave's regularity as the speaker asked direct questions to specific pieces.

"The shortwave's inflections were very quick after each question was asked, which indicates that perhaps the life forms are a bit more responsive when singled out individually.

"When the speaker addressed the Mayan statue, I observed it radiating a light that is best described as a dull-reddish magenta color. The light fully surrounded the Mayan and streamed off a bit in the direction of the microphone, but did not get close to it. this light remained until the session was over."

## Instrumental Transcommunication (ITC)

In 1985 Swiss electronics expert, Klaus Schreiber who, as a result of studying George Meek's Spiricom designs, invented an apparatus he called "Vidicom." The Vidicom consisted of a specially adapted TV, switched on but not attached to an aerial, with a video camera in front of it to capture images that appeared on the screen. One of the first pictures he received was a blurred, fleeting image of a human figure.

Occasionally just voices would come across, telling him how to tune his TV for better reception. A typical session would begin with a TV screen full of dots. Then small ovals would appear one after another, each growing quickly until they disappeared off the screen. Within minutes faces would start to appear along with voices, to the astonishment of Schreiber himself and his visitors.

It wasn't long after Shreiber death in 1988 that his image started appearing on the TV screens of Europe's ITC researchers. Schreiber's friend Martin Wenzel continued his work with some success, but as with Spiricom the Schreiber method, to work effectively, needed to be used by someone with the sensitivity of a psychic and strong mediumistic links with other planes of existence.

In April 1990 George Meek's wife Jeanette died after a long illness. Before she crossed over, however, Meek had asked her to get firmly in mind the names TimeStream (a spiritside sending station linked to a young, leading-edge research laboratory in Luxembourg) and Swejen Salter (the system's operator and research director on the spirit side), Hopefully these memories would act as a homing device once she crossed over, pulling Jeannette to the research station.

It apparently worked; three months after Jeannette's funeral she reportedly had located the TimeStream station and sent the following letter to George via the

Luxembourg computer: "DEAR G.W. – WELL, IT SEEMS THERE ARE STILL PEOPLE WHO DO NOT BELIEVE IN THE CONTACTS YOUR FRIENDS HERE IN LUXEMBOURG ARE HAVING. HENCE I WILL GIVE YOU SOME PERSONAL DETAILS KNOWN ONLY TO YOU AND MOLLY.

"FIRST STORY. IN 1987, END OF APRIL, OUR TENANT DEBBIE CALLED TO SAY HER REFRIGERATOR WAS OFF. IT MUST HAVE BEEN ON A THURSDAY MORNING...

"SECOND STORY. ON APRIL 29, 1987, ANN VALENTIN WROTE A LETTER FORM CALIFORNIA SAYING SHE HAD NOT RECEIVED THE MAGIC OF LIVING FOREVER BOOKLETS SHE HAD ORDERED, BUT INSTEAD HAD RECEIVED A BOX OF HARLEQUIN NOVELS.

"THIRD STORY. JOHN LATHROP SHUTOFF THE ELECTRICITY AT OUR RENTAL HOUSE TO PUT IN THE NEW YARD LIGHT, HE WASN'T DOWN THERE VERY LONG BUT CHARGED $20 SERVICE IN ADDITION TO $40 FOR THE BULBS, PLUS TAX. THE CHARGE SEEMED HIGH.

"DON'T TRY TO EXPLAIN THIS, HONEY, MY NEVER-ENDING LOVE TO YOU. I MISS YOU SO MUCH, BUT I KNOW WE WILL BE TOGETHER. LOVE FOREVER, JEANNETTE DUNCAN MEEK."

To support the validity of the ITC contact, Jeannette had selected three very private items known only to the Meeks and their secretary Molly Philo. The second item about romance novels, in fact, was a complete puzzle even to George.

Upon receiving Jeannette's letter from the Luxembourg team and getting his excitement under control, Meek called Ann Valentin in California to verify item two. Sure enough, a carton of novels had arrived mysteriously in 1987, and to this day no one knows who sent them.

The most exciting and potentially fruitful development is that of communication via computer. Ken Webster of England published a book in which he reported on more than 200 computer contacts with local persons who had died more than three centuries ago.

One of Webster's main contacts was 16th century Englishman Thomas Harden, who had lived in the same house that Webster now resided in, when the town was still named Bristol. From the astral planes, Harden could see Webster's electronic equipment in the living room.

# The Lost Journals of Nikola Tesla

He referred to the computer as a box with a multitude of lights sitting near my chimney. Harden would communicate in old English grammar in a variety of ways – telepathic messages, scribbles on note paper, chalk-written messages on the floor and, most important, computer files written on the display screen and generated on hard disk.

Harden later was reported to have explained to his earth-side colleague Webster that the writing was formed according to his will or his visualization in the "Lightbox." Another interesting feature was that Harden said that he wasn't a discarnate entity, communicating from the beyond. Instead he claimed to be speaking from his own time in the 17th century. So rather then talking with the dead, this seems to be a case of time travel.

During the 1980's psychic researchers became aware of claims that various people had received telephone calls from loved ones after they had died. The calls were usually only of short duration and when investigated did not register on normal telephone monitoring equipment. This subject was extensively covered by D. Scott Rogo in his book *Telephone Calls From The Dead.* (1979).

A husband and wife couple working in Luxembourg between 1985 and 1988 along with helpers from the afterlife, developed two electronic systems which became significantly more reliable and repeatable than the systems developed earlier.

Jules and Maggie Harsch-Fishbach in 1987 established computer contact which allows submission of technical questions with high speed print-out of the carefully considered replies. Also in 1987 they got TV picture sequences of good quality (*Psychic News* February 25th 1995).

By 1993 the research team in the afterlife was able to access the hard drives of computers and leave detailed, computer-scanned images as well as several pages of text. The computer-scanned images were far more detailed and less subject to distortion than the video images. Researchers on earth were able to direct questions to their counterparts on the other side and receive answers by telephone, radio, TV, computer, or fax (Kubris and Macy 1995: 14).

Dominic R Macquarie stated in the November 15, 1997 issue of *Psychic News* that communication between the earth plane and the afterlife is more successful when there is a mediumistic person, who has more than average ectoplasm present. This had earlier been confirmed by Konstantine, Raudive, German Professor E Senkowski and George Meek.

# The Lost Journals of Nikola Tesla

The need to have some form of electromagnetic energy present has always been recognized as an essential component of EVP. Macquarie claims that experimenters since 1963 have obtained better results if they turn on three twelve volt transformers (the kind which change household voltage to lower voltage for portable radios, CD players etc.) within 3 to 4 inches (8-12cms) of each other. They produce a very quiet hum which provides a weak gentle field of electromagnetic energy which can be used by discarnate entities.

"One has always to keep in mind that whilst ectoplasm and electromagnetic energy must be present when communicating with the afterlife, an experimenter who is negative and uses the presumption of futility will be exuding negative energy and will dramatically reduce successful communication," says Macquarie. "This 'experimenter effect' has been found in mediumship, laboratory testing and when using electronic equipment.

"So even though communication can occur through television, radio equipment and the telephone, the clarity of transmission depends on the contact field, the thoughts of those receiving the transmission. It has been discovered at large open meetings, that if a group of people had negative thoughts about ITC, their negative vibrations seriously affected the vibrations coming from the astral plane."

Even though Nikola Tesla in his early years had little patience with those who believed in spirits and unknown psychic abilities, he may have had a change of heart later in his life and after leaving the physical plane. In 1998, a medium by the name of Alice Cromley alleged that she had made contact with the spirit of Tesla through electronic methods similar to what Tesla used.

In a series of communications, all conducted at a secure home in Montreal, Canada, Mrs. Cromley received information concerning Tesla's continued existence after his death and the new discoveries that awaited him on the other side. Tesla was apparently eager to tell those interested in his life and science, not to dismiss ideas that appear supernatural or not of science.

"Physics, extends beyond what is scientifically known today," Tesla communicated. "The future will show that what we now call occult or the supernatural is based on a science not yet developed, but whose first infant steps are being taken as we speak!"

**ABOVE: Tesla was probably the first to experience EVP.**
**BELOW: Bill O'Neil at the Spiricom device.**

# Chapter Six
*UFOs and Electrogravity Propulsion*
*Did Tesla Discover the Secrets of Antigrvity?*

Nikola Tesla has been credited for the creation of much of the technology that we take for granted today. Without the genius of Tesla we would not have radio, television, AC electricity, Tesla coil, flourescent lighting, neon lighting, radio control devices, robotics, x-rays, radar, microwaves and dozens of other amazing inventions.

Because of this, it is no surprise that Tesla also delved into the world of flight and possibly, antigravity. In fact, his last patent in 1928 (# 6,555,114), was for a flying machine that resembled both a helicopter and an airplane. Before he died, Tesla reportedly devised plans for the engine of a spaceship. He called it the anti-electromagnetic field drive or Space Drive.

William R. Lyne writes in *Occult Ether Physics* (Creatopia Productions), that a lecture Tesla prepared for the Institute of Immigrant Welfare (May. 12, 1938), dealt with his Dynamic Theory of Gravity. Tesla said in his lecture that this was: "One of two far reaching discoveries, which I worked out in all details in the years 1893 and 1894."

While researching Tesla's statements, Lyne discovered that more complete statements concerning these discoveries could only be gleaned from scattered and sparse sources, because Tesla's papers are concealed in government vaults for national security reasons.

When Lyne specifically asked for these papers at the National Security Research Center (now the Robert J. Oppenheimer Research Center) in 1979, he was denied access because they were still classified. In his 1938 lecture, Tesla said he was progressing with the work, and hoped to give the theory to the world very soon. The two great discoveries to which Tesla referred, were:

1. The Dynamic Theory of Gravity - which assumed a field of force which accounts for the motions of bodies in space; assumption of this field of force dispenses with the concept of space curvature (ala Einstein); the ether has an indispensable function in the phenomena (of universal gravity, inertia, momentum, and movement of heavenly bodies, as well as all atomic and molecular matter).

# The Lost Journals of Nikola Tesla

2. Environmental Energy - the Discovery of a new physical Truth: there is no energy in matter other than that received from the environment. (Which goes against Einstein's E=mc2). The usual Tesla birthday announcement - on his 79th birthday (1935) - Tesla made a brief reference to the theory saying it applies to molecules and atoms as well as to the largest heavenly bodies, and to "...all matter in the universe in any phase of its existence from its very formation to its ultimate disintegration."

In an article, *Man's Greatest Achievement*, Tesla outlined his Dynamic Theory of Gravity by saying that the luminiferous ether fills all space. The ether is acted upon by the life-giving creative force and is thrown into "infinitesimal whirls" ("micro helices") at near the speed of light, becoming ponderable matter. When the force subsides and motion ceases, matter reverts to the ether (a form of "atomic decay").

Man can harness these processes to: Precipitate matter from the ether. Create whatever he wants with the matter and energy derived. Alter the earth's size. Control earth's seasons (weather control). Guide earth's path through the Universe, like a spaceship. Cause the collisions of planets to produce new suns and stars, heat, and light. Originate and develop life in infinite forms.

When Tesla was 82, instead of speaking at a dinner party, he issued a written statement. Although this was soon after he had been struck by a car, his mind was obviously still capable of mounting an attack on Einstein's theory of relativity:

"I have worked out a dynamic theory of gravity in all details and hope to give this to the world very soon. It explains the causes of this force and the motions of heavenly bodies under its influence so satisfactorily that it will put an end to idle speculations and false conceptions, as that of curved space. According to the relativists, space has a tendency to curvature owing to an inherent property or presence of celestial bodies.

"Granting a semblance of reality to this fantastic idea, it is still very self-contradictory. Every action is accompanied by an equivalent reaction and the effects of the latter are directly opposite to those of the former. Supposing that the bodies act upon the surrounding space causing curvature of the same, it appears to my simple mind that the curved spaces must react on the bodies and, producing the opposite effects, straighten out the curves.

"Since action and reaction are coexistent, it follows that the supposed curvature of space is entirely impossible – However, even if it existed it would not explain the motions of the bodies as observed. Only the existence of a field of force can account for them and its assumption dispenses with space curvature. All literature on this subject is futile and destined to oblivion."

It is a great pity that Tesla never published his dynamic theory of gravity. Modern thinking about gravity suggests that when a heavy object moves it emits gravitational waves that radiate at the speed of light. These gravity waves behave in similar ways to many other types of waves.

Tesla's greatest inventions were all based on the study of waves. He always considered sound, light, heat, X-rays and radio waves to be related phenomena that could be studied using the same sort of maths. His differences with Einstein suggest that he had extended this thinking to gravity.

In the 1980s he was proved to be right. A study of energy loss in a double neutron star pulsar called PSR 1913 + 16 proved that gravity waves exist. Tesla's idea that gravity is a field effect is now taken more seriously than Einstein took it.

Unfortunately, Tesla never revealed what had led him to this conclusion. He never explained his theory of gravitation to the world. The attack he made on Einstein's work was considered outrageous by the scientific establishment of the time, and only now do we have enough understanding of gravity to realize that he was right.

## How to Build a Flying Saucer

Tesla had discovered that the electrostatic emission from the surface of a conductor will always concentrate where the surface curves or even presents an edge. The sharper the curve or edge, the greater the concentration of electron emission. Tesla also observed that an electrostatic charge will flow over the surface of a conductor rather than penetrate it. This is called the Faraday or Skin Effect, discovered by Michael Faraday many years ago.

This also explains the principles of the Faraday Cage which is used in high voltage research labs to protect humans and electrosensitive equipment from harm. According to eyewitness reports of interiors of UFOs, there is a circular column or channel through the center of the vehicle.

This reportedly serves as a superstructure for the rest of the saucer shaped vehicle, and also carries a high voltage, high frequency coil. It is believed to be a resonant transformer which gives the electrostatic and electromagnetic charge to the craft and establishes polarity.

This coil is relative to what is known as a Tesla coil. The Tesla Coil of course, was invented by Tesla in 1891. This column or channel is approximately two feet in diameter and is hollow. On some vehicles this hollow area has a turbine generator in it.

When the vacuum is created on one hemisphere of the craft, the atmospheric pressure is allowed to rush through the tube to drive a sort of turbine electrical generator. Some reports say the extraterrestrials use this system as stationary power plants for electrical energy on their planets as well.

The eyes of the craft are arranged by electro-optic lenses placed at quadrants or wherever they wish to see from. The screen-like monitors are placed on a console where the navigator can observe all areas around and about the vehicle at the same time. This includes the magnification lenses which are used without changing positions.

There are also windows about elbow level and about one foot through or thick. This distance would have to be in view of the four or more walls or plates of the capacitor hulls making up the major portion of the craft. The windows have an iris type of shutter so that when it is closed, it allows electrostatic charge to flow evenly.

## Dr T. Townsend Brown and Electrogravitics

The idea of using high voltage electricity as a means of propulsion is not new. Tesla laid the groundwork in the late 19th century which was then continued by such notables as Thomas Townsend Brown, who discovered in 1923 what was later called the Biefeld -Brown Effect.

Thomas Townsend Brown, was a physics student of Dr. Paul Alfred Biefeld at the California Institute for Advanced Studies. Brown noticed that when he had two plates carrying high voltages of direct current separated by a dielectric, the negative electrode moved by itself in the direction of the positive plate. In other words, Townsend Brown discovered that it is possible to create an artificial gravity field by charging an electrical capacitor to a high-voltage.

He built a special capacitor which utilized a heavy, high charge-accumulating (high K-factor) dielectric material between its plates and found that when charges with between 70,000 to 300,000 volts, it would move in the direction of its positive pole. When oriented with its positive side up, it would proceed to lose about one percent of it's weight.

He attributed this motion to an electrostatically-induced gravity field acting between the capacitor's oppositely charged plates. By 1958, he had succeeded in developing a 15 inch diameter model saucer that could lift over 110% of its weight. Brown's experiments had launched a new field of investigation which came to be known as Electrogravitics, the technology of controlling gravity through the use of high-voltage electric charge.

As early as 1952, an Air Force major general witnessed a demonstration in which Brown flew a pair of 18 inch disc airfoils suspended from opposite ends of a rotatable arm. When electrified with 50,000 volts, they circuited at a speed of 12 miles per hour.

About a year later, he flew a set of 3 foot diameter saucers for some Air Force officials and representatives from a number of major aircraft companies. When energized with 150,000 volts, the discs sped around the 50 foot diameter course so fast that the subject was immediately classified.

*Interavia* magazine later reported that the discs could attain speeds of several hundred miles per hour when charged with several hundred thousand volts. Brown's discs were charged with a high positive voltage, on a wire, running along their leading edge and a high negative voltage, on a wire, running along their trailing edge.

As the wires ionized the air around them, a dense cloud of positive ions would form ahead of the craft and corresponding cloud of negative ions would form behind the craft. Brown's research indicated that, like the charged plates of his capacitors, these ion clouds induced a gravitational force directed in the minus to plus direction.

As the disc moved forward in the response to its self generated gravity field, it would carry with it its positive and negative ion clouds and their associated electrogravity gradient. Consequently, the discs would ride their advancing gravity wave much like surfers ride an ocean wave.

Dr. Mason Rose, one of Townsend's colleagues, described the discs principle of operation as follows:

"The saucers made by Brown have no propellers, no jets, no moving parts at all. They create a modification of the gravitational field around themselves, which is

Patent #3,322,374          5-30-67

## MAGNETOHYDRODYNAMIC PROPULSION DEVICE

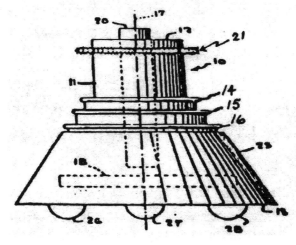

**ABOVE: J. Frank King, a colleague of T. Townsend Brown, patented a magnetohydrodynamic propulsion device. Note the similarities in design to the Adamski flying saucer.**

analogous to putting them on the incline of a hill. They act like a surfboard on a wave. . . the electrogravitational saucer creates its own hill, which is a local distortion of the gravitational field, then it takes this hill with it in any chosen direction and at any rate.

"The occupants of one of [Brown's] saucers would feel no stress at all no matter how sharp the turn or how great the acceleration. This is because the ship and its occupants and the load are all responding equally to the wave-like distortion of the local gravitation field."

Although skeptics at first thought that the discs were propelled by more mundane effects such as the pressure of negative ions striking the positive electrode. Brown later carried out vacuum chamber tests which proved that a force was present even in the absence of such ion thrust.

He did not offer a theory to explain this unconventional electrogravitic phenomenon; except to say that it was predicted neither by general relativity nor by modern theories of electromagnetism. However, recent advances in theoretical physics provide a rather straightforward explanation of the principle.

According to the novel physics of subquantum kinetics, gravity potential can adopt two polarities, instead of one. Not only can a gravity field exist in the form of a matter-attracting gravity potential well, as standard physics teaches, but it can also exist in the form of a matter repelling gravity potential hill.

Moreover, it predicts that these gravity polarities should be directly matched with electrical polarity; positively charged particles such as protons generating gravity wells and negatively charged particles such as electrons generating gravity hills.

Thus contrary to conventional theory, the electron produces a matter-repelling gravity field. Electrical neutral matter remains gravitationally attractive because of the proton's G-well marginally dominates the electron's G-hill. Consequently, subquantum kinetics predicts that the negative ion cloud behind Brown's disc should form a matter repelling gravity hill while the positive ion cloud ahead of the disc should form a matter attracting gravity well.

As increasing voltage is applied to the disc, the gravity potential hill and well become increasing prominent and the gravity potential gradient between them increasing steep. In Rose's terminology, the craft would find itself on the incline of a gravitational hill. Since gravity force is known to increase in accordance with the steepness of such a  gravity potential slope,  increased voltage would induce an increasingly strong gravity force on the disc and would act in the direction of the positive ion cloud. The disc would behave as if it was being tugged by a very strong gravitational field emanating from an invisible planet sized mass positioned beyond its positive pole.

Early in 1952 Brown had put together a proposal, code named Project Winterhaven, which suggested that the military developed an antigravity combat saucer with Mach-3 capability. The 1956 intelligence study entitled *Electrogravitics Systems: An Explanation of Electrostatic Motion, Dynamic Counterbary and Barycentric Control*, prepared by the private aviation intelligence firm, Aviation Studies International Ltd.,indicates that as early as November 1954 the Air Force had begun plans to fund research that would accomplish Project Winterhaven's objectives.

The study, originally classified Confidential, mentions the name of more than ten major aircraft companies which were actively involved in the electrogravitics research in an attempt to duplicate or extend Brown's seminal work. Additional information is to be found in another aviation intelligence report entitled: *The Gravitics Situation*. Unfortunately, due to the militaries TOP SECRET classification, Townsend Brown's work has not appeared in any physics or science publications that can be accessed.

## Article Reveals Government Research

Because of the influence of such pioneers as Tesla and T. Townsend Brown, the research and development of antigravity devices has been ongoing for a number of years. The June 1957 issue of *Mechanic's Illustrated* featured an article by G. Harry Stine entitled: *Conquest of Space*. Stine, the Chief of Navy Range Operations at White Sands Proving Grounds, makes it perfectly clear that the military was extremely interested in antigravity research.

> There is a good chance that the rocket will be obsolete for space travel within 50 years. Some of us have been concentrating on the development of the rocket as the possible power plant for outer space propulsion. We've fired a lot of rockets and we've proved that they will work well in outer space. We've also learned a lot about

what's out there by using rockets. And probably we will take the first few faltering steps into space with rocket power plants.

But recent discoveries indicate that the spaceship of the future may be powered by anti-gravity devices. These, instead of using brute force to overcome gravity, will use the force of gravity itself much as an airplane uses the air to make it fly.

Sir William Crookes, the English scientist who developed the cathode-ray tube we now use for television, made extensive investigations of levitation phenomena - a field that once belonged to vaudeville magicians. Scientists, reasoning that if they believed his reports of weird green glows in vacuum tubes they should also look into Crookes' levitation studies, have been making slow but steady progress.

Others have been investigating the fields of gravitic isotopes, jet electron streams, and the mechanics of the electron shells of atoms. Townsend T. Brown, an American investigator, has gone even further than that. There are rumors that Brown has developed a real antigravity machine. There are many firms working on the problems of antigravity - the Glenn L. Martin Co., Bell Aircraft, General Electric, Sperry-Rand Corp. and others.

Rumors have been circulating that scientists have built disc airfoils two feet in diameter incorporating a variation of the simple two-plate electrical condenser (capacitor), which charged to a potential of 50,000 volts, has achieved a speed of seventeen feet per second with a total energy input of fifty watts.

A three-foot diameter disc airfoil charged to 150 Kilovolts turned out such an amazing performance that the whole thing was immediately classified. Flame-jet generators, making use of the electrostatic charge discovered in rocket exhausts, have been developed which will supply charges up to 15 million volts.

Several important things have been discovered with regard to gravity propulsion. For one, the propulsive force doesn't act on only one part of the ship it is pushing; it acts on all parts within the gravity field created by the gravitic drive. It probably is not limited to the speed of light.

# The Lost Journals of Nikola Tesla

Gravity-powered vehicles have apparently changed direction, accelerated rapidly at very high g's and stopped abruptly without any heavy stresses being experienced by the measuring devices aboard the vehicle and within the gravity-propulsion field. This control is done by changing the direction, intensity and polarity of the charge on the condenser plates of the drive unit, a fairly simple task for scientists.

Sounds incredible, doesn't it? But the information comes from reliable sources. We are licking the problems of gravity. Indications are that we are on the verge of tapping a brand new group of electrical waves which link electricity and gravity. Electronic engineers have taken the electrical coil and used it as a link between electricity and electro-magnetism, thus giving us a science of electromagnetic's which in turn has given us such things as radio, television, radar and the like.

Now, gravity researchers seem to think that the condenser will open up the science of electrogravitics. Soon we may be able to eliminate gravity as a structural, dynamic and medical problem.

Although we will probably use rocket power to make our first explorations into space, the chances are now pretty good that this will not always be the case. In 50 years we may travel to the moon, the planets or even the stars propelled by the harnessed forces of gravity.

If this seems fantastic, remember that the rocket and the idea of a trip to the moon was fantastic twenty years ago. Fifty years ago the idea of commercial air travel was utter nonsense.

With gravitic spaceships, we may travel to the moon in less than an hour, to the planets in less than a day or to the stars themselves in a matter of months. We may be able to do it in absolute comfort without the problems of zero-gravity or high accelerations.

The idea of the rocket becoming obsolete is not a happy idea, particularly when so much work has been done on rockets. If a better method comes along, why shed tears? After all, our basic goal is to travel and explore in space and it doesn't make much difference how we do it.

# The Lost Journals of Nikola Tesla

## Is Antigravity Already in Use?

Recently an article appeared in *Jane's Aviation Weekly* that stated the B-2 Stealth Nuclear-Strike Bomber is in fact, currently using an electrogravitic propulsion system. Paul A. LaViolette has done considerable study on the use of electrogravitic technology by the U.S. Air Force, which has conducted secret Black Project research on the matter since late 1954.

LaViolette contends that electrogravitics may have been put to practical use in the B-2 Advanced Technology Bomber to provide an exotic auxiliary mode of propulsion. This conclusion is based on the recent disclosure that the B-2 charges both its wing leading edge and jet exhaust stream to a high voltage.

Positive ions emitted from its wing leading edge would produce a positively charged parabolic ion sheath ahead of the craft while negative ions injected into it's exhaust stream would set up a trailing negative space charge with a potential difference in excess of 15 million volts.

According to electrogravitic research carried out by Tesla and T. Townsend Brown, such a differential space charge would set up an artificial gravity field that would induce a reactionless force on the aircraft in the direction of the positive pole.

An electrogravitic drive of this sort could allow the B-2 to function with over-unity propulsion efficiency when cruising at supersonic velocities. On March 9, 1992, *Aviation Week And Space Technology* magazine made a surprising disclosure that the B-2 electrostatically charges its exhaust stream and the leading edges of its wing-like body.

Those familiar with the research of Tesla in the early 20th century will quickly realize that this is tantamount to stating that the B-2 is able to function as an antigravity aircraft. *Aviation Week* obtained their information about the B-2 from a small group of renegade west coast scientists and engineers who were formerly associated with black research projects.

In making these disclosures, these scientists broke a code of silence that rivals the Mafia's. They took the risk because they felt that it was important for economic reasons that efforts be made to declassify certain black technologies for commercial use.

Two of these individuals said that their civil rights had been blatantly abused (in the name of security) either to keep them quiet or to prevent them from leaving the tightly controlled black research and development community. Although the scientists mentioned nothing about electrogravitics in their *Aviation Week* disclosure about the B-2, they did admit to the existence of very dramatic, classified technologies applicable to aircraft control and propulsion.

They were especially hesitant to discuss these projects, noting that they are very secret. One of them commented: "Besides, it would take about 20 hours to explain the principles, and very few people would understand them anyway."

Apparently what he meant is that this aircraft control and propulsion technology is based on principles that go beyond what is currently known and understood by most academic physicists. That is with the exception of two geniuses who developed the original ideas for high voltage electric drives decades ago.

It must be also considered that the B-2 is now no longer the only aircraft to use such technologies. Since that time an entire generation of black budget secret aircraft may have been developed with electrogravitic systems.

## Art Bell's Mysterious Metal — The Key to Antigravity

The suggestion that UFOs could be manmade flying machines using exotic technologies is not new to the study of unidentified flying objects. In the 1950's several researchers in Europe claimed that Tesla and Marconi had secretly built and tested operational antigravity aircraft. Using electrogravitic drives, these experimental aircraft were eventually based out of a secret location in South America.

Allegedly, Nazi Germany got a hold of this technology and produced several antigravity flying saucers of their own. Fortunately, by the time Hitler decided to dedicate more time and funds to the Nazi flying saucer project, the war was almost over for the Germans. Of course by that time Tesla had passed away, but it is almost certain that he would have been horrified by the use of his invention by the Germans.

Early evidence for these anecdotal tales was scant and consisted almost entirely of discovered research papers and a few photos of similarly shaped UFOs. As has been already noted in this book, early UFO contactees such as George Adamski and Howard Menger witnessed and even photographed UFOs that bore a striking resemblance to the small discs built by T. Townsend Brown.

# The Lost Journals of Nikola Tesla

Could these UFOs actually be manmade machines flown by humans? Or were extraterrestrials flying around in spacecraft utilizing similar technology as that discovered by Tesla and Brown?

In 1996, late night radio host Art Bell received a package containing bits of metal that the sender claimed was taken from the crashed UFO found near Roswell, New Mexico in 1947. Could these unassuming pieces of metal be the evidence that proved the reality of UFOs and their use of electrogravitic technology? The pieces of metal seemed almost too good to be true and Bell was at first skeptical because of similar past hoaxes involving alleged parts from UFOs.

Bell sent a few samples to Linda Moulton Howe, who promptly had the metal analyzed. Using Wave Dispersive Spectroscopy, It was discovered that the metal was made up of a magnesium zinc alloy with pure bismuth layers. There was a range from 97 to about 97 - ½ % magnesium and 3% to 2 - ½ % zinc in each of those 100 to 200micron layers of the magnesium zinc, so the metal was almost entirely magnesium with about 3% zinc.

The pure bismuth layers were one to four microns thick in a slightly wavy pattern and nothing else but bismuth was found. No oxygen was found, no zirconium, no other elements - just these three.

High energy experiments conducted on the unusual metal indicated a tendency for lateral movement. Unfortunately, this research has not resulted in any solid conclusions at this time.

After this information was broadcast on Art's show, Howe received a fax from a listener named Dan who indicated he had professional knowledge that would relate the material to antigravity. He had worked from 1973 to 1980 for an organization called Aeronautical Systems Division at Edwards Air Force Base in California with some assignments at Wright Patterson in Ohio.

Dan received bachelors degrees in physics, aerospace engineering and computer science from California Polytechnic State University, a masters degrees in computer science and aerospace engineering from the University of California at Berkley and then received his Ph.D. in physics in 1974 after he had already begun work as a civilian scientist for the Air Force.

Dan told Howe that he had been involved in aeronautical engineering and evaluations when he first saw metal similar to what was sent to Art bell. The metal supposedly was used in a electrogravitic capacity. In the case of bismuth, its basically a diamagnetic material which means it tends to repel a magnetic field.

# The Lost Journals of Nikola Tesla

"There were very strange things that were bound with bismuth as basically positive charges were added to it, you know, putting a field, a positive electron field into the bismuth," Dan said to Howe. "As a matter of fact they were very dramatic, some of the things that they found. A lot of this goes all the way back to 1917 with Nikola Tesla and his discoveries of electrical fields and gravity."

Howe wanted to know what was the most dramatic thing that would happen as the positive flow was increased into bismuth. Dan's answer was that basically there would be a mass reduction to the point where it could come to zero and actually rise into the air, creating a lifting body.

A now defunct UFO group in England claimed that one of their members had conducted experiments with dissimilar metals in the 1970's. He used two disks of the same dimension and thickness but of two different materials, copper and zinc. The disks were kept very close together and rotated in opposite directions. The claim was they levitated when spun, though the comment did not specify the requirement for high voltage as in the case of the Biefeld/Brown effect.

It was simply rotation of mass which is more consistent with Otis T. Carr, Bruce DePalma and Dr. Harold Aspden, with their claims of anomalous inertial or gravitic effects associated with rotating mass.

An interesting story was told at the recent Low Level Energy Conference by Michael Roberts, President of the Association for Push Gravity Research. One day a few years ago, he got a phone call at his home in Waco. It was from a fellow who had stopped in Waco and wanted to meet Michael at a local mall.

Michael drove out to the mall and the man was parked, in his late model Jeep in a remote section of the parking lot. They shook hands and talked a bit. The man said he would like to show Michael what he had been working on.

The Jeep engine was off, the vehicle was put in neutral and was not braked in anyway. Michael was asked to push the vehicle. He did so with both hands, meeting an expected amount of resistance before he got it moving.

The man got in and braked the vehicle. He then showed Michael four mystery boxes (each about 12" X 6" X 4"), mounted in the top of each wheel well of the Jeep. Each box had an electrical cable that led under the hood. Michael was not allowed to see under the hood.

Immediately after the push test, the man got in the Jeep and flicked a toggle switch which had been installed under the dashboard. Michael was then asked to push the Jeep again, this time it moved with the light touch of one hand. The man would say nothing about how this miracle was accomplished, he just wanted to show Michael that it was possible to achieve an antigravity effect using electricity.

One possible explanation may be that the four boxes acted to provide a stabilized buoyancy type field, like pontoons on a boat. The use of only one would deflect the incoming gravity in one localized area, thus creating an imbalance. Whereas one unit over each wheel would equally distribute the deflection around the center of mass of the Jeep.

The book *Occult Ether Physics: Tesla's Hidden Space Propulsion System And The Conspiracy To Conceal It*, concentrates on the 19th century Aether science leading up to Tesla's discovery of electro-propulsion. Tesla's holy grail was to build his electric flying machine, and to draw some of the environmental energy out of the cosmos.

This plan involved a theory of radioactivity under development by Tesla in the 1890s, which entirely presaged and conflicted with currently accepted Relativism, quantum mechanics, and nuclear energy theories. To Tesla, so-called atomic energy was in fact the result of environmental energy emanating from the cosmos, and made known to us via radioactive matter. This matter, Tesla said, had the peculiar property of resonating and reacting with ubiquitous cosmic radiation.

The cosmic radiation of which Tesla spoke was of much higher frequency than what we call radioactive emanations. Tesla believed that these were the result of a step-down process, in which certain peculiar matter reacts to and converts ubiquitous, omnidirectional cosmic radiation.

Today, we call this zero point radiation (ZPR), from higher frequencies, to lower, more useful and appropriate frequencies, such as gamma, x-ray, ultraviolet, visible, infrared radiation, as well as magnetism and even electrical current. These step-down frequencies are much easier to detect and measure than the ZPR.

The existence of the ZPR was well known to Tesla in the 1890s, but it was not until recently that it became scientifically accepted as a proven fact. This radiation is of such high frequency that it normally passes through space, the earth, and our bodies without harm or incident, in constant equilibrium, because its short wavelengths do not normally react or resonate with the atoms of most matter.

It is radioactive matter, according to Tesla, which has a peculiar atomic structure which reacts with this radiation to produce radioactivity. Atomic energy, to Tesla, comes from the ZPR, not atoms. If a lump of radium could be shielded from the effects of the ZPR, said Tesla, it would show no radioactivity.

# The Lost Journals of Nikola Tesla

Most naturally radioactive elements are dense and unstable, that is, they are said by the Relativists to decay as radiation is emitted, to elements of lower atomic numbers. The Relativists, with whom Tesla vehemently disagreed, believe that naturally radioactive elements spontaneously lose mass in the process of such decay, so that the energy released as radioactivity, is equivalent to the lost mass according to Einstein's equation, $E=mc2$.

If non-radioactive elements are converted into radioactive elements by the forces of nature, what are these processes? In a *New York Times* article of July 11, 1937 (pg.13, col.2), in one of Tesla's famous birthday announcements, Tesla stated that he had developed a process for the manufacture of radium (transmutation from other elements),which was so efficient that it could be sold for $1.00 per pound.

He also announced that he had absolutely developed a system for the interstellar transmission of energy. He said he had been working in several laboratories, but refused to disclose their locations.

His working model, he said, "...employs more than three dozen of my inventions. It is a complex apparatus, an agglomeration of parts. It could convey several thousand units of horsepower to other planets, regardless of the distance. Traveling through a channel of less than one-half of one-millionth of a centimeter." Further, he said, "This is not an experiment. I have built, demonstrated and used it. Only a little time will pass before I can give it to the world."

These facts demonstrate that even in his 80s, Tesla was involved in secret research at several undisclosed laboratories, on technology which even today remains highly classified. Technology that is only now being fully understood and secretly utilized.

## The Tesla Flying Saucer

Bill Jones, writing for *The UFO Enigma*, the newsletter for the UFO Study Group of greater St. Louis, comments that Tesla did the basic research for constructing electromagnetic field lift-and-drive aircraft/spacecraft. From 1891 to 1893, he gave a set of lectures and demonstrations to groups of electrical engineers.

# The Lost Journals of Nikola Tesla

As part of each show, Tesla stood in the middle of the stage, using his 6' 6" height, with an assistant on either side, each seven feet away. All three men wore thick cork or rubber shoe soles to avoid being electrically grounded. Each assistant held a wire, part of a high voltage, low current circuit.

When Tesla raised his arms to each side, violet colored electricity jumped harmlessly across the gaps between the men. At high voltage and frequency in this arrangement, electricity flows over a surface, even the skin, rather than into it. This is a basic circuit which could be used by aircraft/spacecraft.

The hull is best made double, of thin, machinable, slightly flexible ceramic. This becomes a good electrical insulator, has no fire danger, resists any damaging effects of severe heat and cold, and has the hardness of armor, besides being easy for magnetic fields to pass through.

The inner hull is covered on it's outside by wedge shaped thin metal sheets of copper or aluminum, bonded to the ceramic. Each sheet is three to four feet wide at the horizontal rim of the hull and tapers to a few inches wide at the top of the hull for the top set of metal sheets, or at the bottom for the bottom set of sheets. Each sheet is separated on either side from the next sheet by 1 or 2 inches of uncovered ceramic hull.

The top set of sheets and bottom set of sheets are separated by about 6 inches of uncovered ceramic hull around the horizontal rim of the hull. The outer hull protects these sheets from being short-circuited by wind blown metal foil (Air Force radar confusing chaff), heavy rain or concentrations of gasoline or kerosene fumes.

If unshielded, fuel fumes could be electrostatically attracted to the hull sheets, burn and form carbon deposits across the insulating gaps between the sheets, causing a short-circuit. The space, the outer hull with a slight negative charge, would absorb hits from micro-meteorites and cosmic rays (protons moving at near the speed of light).

Any danger of this type that doesn't already have a negative electric charge would get a negative charge in hitting the outer hull, and be repelled by the metal sheets before it could hit the inner hull. The hull can be made in a variety of shapes; sphere, football, disc, or streamlined rectangle or triangle, as long as these metal sheets, "are of considerable area and arranged along ideal enveloping surfaces of very large radii of curvature," p. 85. *My Inventions*, by Nikola Tesla.

Tesla's concept of a electrogravitic aircraft originally conceived in 1919. "I am now planning aerial machines devoid of sustaining planes, ailerons, propellers and other external attachments, which will be capable of immense speeds."

# The Lost Journals of Nikola Tesla

The power plant for this machine can be a nuclear fission or fusion reactor for long range and long-term use to run a steam engine which turns the generators. A short range machine can use a hydrogen oxygen fuel cell to run a low-voltage motor to turn the generators, occasionally recharging by hovering next to high voltage power lines and using antennas mounted on the outer hull to take in the electricity. The short-range machine can also have electricity beamed to it from a generating plant on a long-range aircraft/spacecraft or on the ground.

One standard for the generators is to have the same number of magnets as field coils. Tesla's preferred design was a thin disc holding 480 magnets with 480 field coils wired in series surrounding it in close tolerance. At 50 revolutions per minute, it produces 19,400 cycles per second.

The electricity is fed into a number of large capacitors, one for each metal sheet. An automatic switch, adjustable in timing by the pilot, closes, and as the electricity jumps across the switch, back and forth, it raises it's own frequency a switch being used for each capacitor.

The electricity goes into a Tesla transformer; again, one transformer for each capacitor. In an oil tank to insulate the windings and for cooling, and supported internally by wood, or plastic, pipe and fittings, each Tesla transformer looks like a short wider pipe that is moved along a longer, narrower pipe by an insulated non-electric cable handle. The short pipe, the primary, is six to ten windings (loops) of wire connected in series to the long pipe. The secondary is 460 to 600 windings, at the low voltage and frequency end.

The insulated non-electric cable handle is used through a set of automatic controls to move the primary coil to various places on the secondary coil. This is the frequency control. The secondary coil has a low frequency and voltage end and a maximum voltage and frequency end. The greater the frequency the electricity, the more it pushes against the earth's electrostatic and electromagnetic fields.

The electricity comes out of the transformer at the high voltage end and goes by wire through the ceramic hull to the wide end of the metal sheet. The electricity jumps out on and flows over the metal sheet, giving off a very strong electromagnetic field, controlled by the transformer. At the narrow end of the metal sheet, most of the high-voltage push having been given off, the electricity goes back by wire through the hull to a circuit breaker box (emergency shut off).

# The Lost Journals of Nikola Tesla

In bright sunlight, the aircraft/spacecraft may seem surrounded by hot air, a slight magnetic distortion of the light. In semi-darkness and night, the metal sheets glow, even through the thin ceramic outer hull, with different colors. The visible light is a by-product of the electricity flowing over the metal sheets, according to the frequencies used.

Descending, landing or just starting to lift from the ground, the transformer primaries are near the secondary weak ends and therefore, the bottom set of sheets glow a misty red. Red may also appear at the front of the machine when it is moving forward fast, lessening resistance up front.

Orange appears for slow speed. Orange-yellow are for airplane-type speeds. Green and blue are for higher speeds. With a capacitor addition, making it oversized for the circuit, the blue becomes bright white, like a searchlight, with possible risk of damaging the metal sheets involved.

The highest visible frequency is violet, like Tesla's stage demonstrations, used for the highest speed along with the bright white. The colors are nearly coherent, of a single frequency, like a laser. A machine built with a set of super conducting magnets would simplify and reduce electricity needs from a vehicle's transformer circuits to the point of flying along efficiently and hovering with very little waste of electricity.

When Tesla was developing arc lights to run on alternating current, there was a bothersome high-pitched whine, whistle, or buzz, due to the electrodes rapidly heating and cooling. Tesla put this noise in the ultrasonic range with the special transformer already mentioned. The aircraft/spacecraft gives off such noises when working at low frequencies.

Timing is important in the operation of this machine. For every three metal sheets, when the middle one is briefly turned off, the sheet on either side is energized, giving off the magnetic field. The next instant, the middle sheet is energized, while the sheet on either side is briefly turned off.

There is a time delay in the capacitors recharging themselves, so at any time, half of all the metal sheets are energized and the other half are recharging, alternating all around the inner hull. This balances the machine, giving it very good stability. This balance is less when fewer of the circuits are in use.

At a fairly close range, the aircraft/spacecraft produces heating of persons and objects on the ground; but by hovering over an area at low altitude for maybe five or ten minutes, the machine also produces a column of very cold air down to the ground.  As air molecules get into the strong magnetic fields that  the machine is  transmitting out, the air molecules become polarized and from lines, or strings, of air molecules.

The  normal  movement of the air is stopped, and there is suddenly a lot more room for air molecules in this area, so more air pours in.  This expansion and the lack of normal air motion make the area intensely cold. This is also the reason that the aircraft/spacecraft can fly at supersonic speeds without making sonic booms.

As  air flows over  the hull, top  and  bottom, the air molecules form lines as they  go through  the  magnetic fields of the metal sheet circuits.  As the air molecules are left behind, they keep their line arrangements for a short time, long enough to cancel out the sonic boom shock waves.

Outside the  earth's magnetic field, another propulsion  system must be used, which relies on the first. You may have read of particle accelerators, or cyclotrons, or atom smashers. A particle accelerator is a circular  loop of pipe that, in cross-section, is oval.

In a physics laboratory, most of the air in it is pumped out. The pipe loop  is given a static electric charge, a small amount of  hydrogen or other  gas is given the same electric charge  so  the particles won't stick to the pipe. A set of electromagnets  all around the pipe  loop  turn on and off, one after the other, pushing with one magnetic pole and pulling with the  next, until those gas particles are racing  around the pipe loop at nearly  the speed  of light.

Centrifugal force  makes  the  particles speed closer to the outside edge of the pipe loop, still within the pipe.  The particles break down into electrons, or light and other  wavelengths, protons or cosmic rays, and  neutrons  if more than hydrogen  is  put  in  the accelerator.

At least two particle accelerators are used to balance each other and counter each other's tendency to  make the craft spin. Otherwise, the machine  would tend  to want to  start spinning, following the direction of the force being applied to the particles. The accelerators push in opposite directions.

The high speed particles go  out  through  straight  lengths of  pipe, charged like the loops and in speeding out into space, push the machine along. Doors control which  pipes the particles leave from.  This allows very  long range  acceleration and later deceleration at normal (earth) gravity. This avoids the  severe  problems of weightlessness,  including lowered physical abilities of the crew. It is possible to use straight-line particle accelerators, even as few as one per machine, but these don't seem as able to get the best machine speed for the least amount of particles pushed out.

Using a constant acceleration of 32.2 feet per second provides earth normal gravity in deep space and only two gravities of stress in leaving the earth's gravity field. It takes, not counting air resistance, 18 minutes, 58.9521636 seconds to reach the 25,000 miles per hour speed to leave the earth's gravity field.

A shortwave radio can be used to find the exact frequencies that an aircraft/spacecraft is using, for each of the colors it may show, a color television can show the same overall color frequency that the nearby, but not extremely close, craft is using. This is limited in its use, as a machine traveling at the speed of a jet airliner may broadcast in a frequency range usually used for radar sets.

The craft circuits would tend to override lower voltage electric circuits within and near their electromagnetic fields. One source briefly mentioned a 1941 incident, where a shortwave radio was used to override automobile ignition systems, up to three miles away. How many UFO encounters have been reported in which automobile ignition systems have suddenly stopped?

## Tesla's Connection to Project Rainbow

Nikola Tesla has recently been the subject of controversy due to the claims of Al Bielek and Preston Nichols. These men have reported in a number of books and articles that Tesla was involved in one of the most disputed mysteries of World War II, The Philadelphia Experiment.

The Philadelphia Experiment, otherwise known as Project Rainbow, was allegedly an attempt by the Navy to create a ship that could not be detected by magnetic mines and or radar. However, its results were said to be far different and much more dangerous than the Navy ever expected.

In the early 1930's, the University of Chicago investigated the possibility of invisibility through the use of electricity. This project was later moved to Princeton's Institute of Advanced Studies where it was named Project Rainbow (project invisibility), and was founded in 1936.

Nicola Tesla was named Director of the project. Tesla was given anything that was required by him for the testing of the project. Tesla required and was given a navy battle ship on which the experiments were to be tested. The first test of invisibility occurred in 1940 and was slated as a full success when a navy ship with no crew on board vanished from this plane of existence.

The basic design, had two large Tesla coils (electromagnets) placed on each hull of the ship. The coils are turned on in a special sequence and their magnetic force is so powerful that they warp gravity itself.

Based in part on Tesla's earlier electrogravitic experiments, Project Rainbow proved to be far more dangerous than was originally conceived. Al Bielek claims that Tesla began to have doubts about the safety of the experiment due to his communications with extraterrestrials.

"Tesla had a press announcement in 1923 where he stated he was talking with ET's off planet. Now after he retired from RCA he maintained a laboratory in his living quarters at the Hotel New Yorker. Unknown to most people he had a second laboratory which apparently was his main one on top of the Waldorf Astoria on the top floor and both penthouse towers.

"He maintained a transmitter setup on the Waldorf; and his receiving setup, his receiving antennas and receivers which had been built by RCA under his direction, were on the New Yorker. And I know two people who said they were working with Tesla, during that period, that he was using that equipment, he was talking with somebody, virtually every day, and one of them was emphatic: it was someone off planet. In plain language, he was communicating with ET's."

Tesla stated that there would be a serious problem with personnel if anyone were to enter the ship while the gauss coils were turned on and the Electro Magnetic radiation would damage them within this reality. He said in numerous occasions that he was in contact with extraterrestrials and that the ET's had confirmed that there would be a problem with the experiment.

Tesla wanted to clarify the problem before any farther experiments would begin. However the Navy said no, they were fighting a war and wanted immediate results. On the second experiment, Tesla, fearing that there would be people hurt or killed in the experiment, decided to sabotage the 1942 test. He de-tuned the equipment so nothing would work and the test failed. Tesla resigned in March 1942 and left the project.

In July 1943, the destroyer U.S.S. Eldridge pulled into the Delaware Bay area for a United States Naval experiment that involved the task of making the ship invisible using Tesla technology. The project's official name was *Project Rainbow,* but is more commonly known as the Philadelphia Experiment.

# Chapter Seven
## *Free Energy - Fact or Fiction?*

While in college Tesla thought it could be possible to operate an electrical motor without sparking brushes. He was told by the professor that such a motor would require perpetual motion and was therefore impossible. Tesla was determined to prove him wrong.

In the 1880's, despite his professors scoffs, Tesla patented the alternating current generator, motor, and transformer. During the 1890's he intensively investigated other methods of power generation including a charged particle collector patented in 1901.

When the *New York Times* in June of 1902 carried a story about an inventor who claimed he had invented an electrical generator that did not require a prime mover in the form of an external fuel supply, Tesla wrote a friend that he had already invented such a device.

Tesla claimed the invention was an electrical generator that would not consume any fuel. Such a generator would be its own prime mover and was utterly impossible according to modern scientists.

Ninety to a hundred years ago, everybody knew that a heavier-than-air machine could not possibly fly. It would violate the laws of physics. This was the learned opinion of practically all of the so-called experts on the matter.

For example, Simon Newcomb declared in 1901: "The demonstration that no possible combination of known substances, known forms of machinery and known forms of force, can be united in a practical machine by which man shall fly long distances through the air."

Fortunately, a few people such as the Wright Brothers wouldn't accept such pronouncements as the final word. Now we take heavier than air flight for granted. Today, orthodox physicists and other scientists are saying similar things against the idea of free energy technologies.

They use negative terms such as pseudoscience and perpetual motion, and citing physical laws which assert that energy cannot be created or destroyed (1st law of thermodynamics), and there is always a decrease in useful energy (2nd law of thermodynamics).

Free energy inventions are devices which can tap a seemingly unlimited supply of energy from the universe, without burning any kind of fuel, creating the perfect solution to the worldwide energy crisis and its associated pollution, degradation, and depletion of the environment. Most free energy devices probably do not create energy, but rather tap into existing natural energy sources by various forms of induction.

Unlike solar or wind devices, free energy devices need little or no energy storage capacity, because they can tap as much energy as needed when needed. Properly designed, free energy devices do not have any limitations.

In *The Brooklyn Eagle* newspaper, Tesla announced, on July 10th, 1931, that: "I have harnessed the cosmic rays and caused them to operate a motive device." Later on in the same article he said that: "More than 25 years ago I began my efforts to harness the cosmic rays and I can now state that I have succeeded."

In 1933, he made the same assertion in an article for the *New York American*, under the lead in: *Device to Harness Cosmic Energy Claimed by Tesla*.

"This new power for the driving of the world's machinery will be derived from the energy which operates the universe, the cosmic energy, whose central source for the earth is the sun and which is everywhere present in unlimited quantities." Dating back more than 25 years ago from 1933 would mean that the device Tesla was speaking about must have been built before 1908. Almost certainly the idea had occurred to Tesla years earlier. More precise information is available through his correspondence now located in the Columbia University Library's collection.

## Electricity Without Burning Fuel

Writing on June 10th, 1902 to his friend Robert U. Johnson, editor of *Century Magazine*, Tesla included a clipping from the previous day's *New York Herald* about Clemente Figueras, a woods and forest engineer in Las Palmas, capital of the Canary Islands, who had invented a device for generating electricity without burning fuel.

What became of Figueras and his fuel-less generator is not known, but this announcement in the paper prompted Tesla, in his letter to Johnson, to claim he had already developed such a device and had revealed the underlying physical laws.

Other U.S. patents have been filed: (#3,811,058, #3,879,622, and #4,151,4310), for example, for motors that run exclusively on permanent energy, seemingly tapping into energy circulating through the earth's magnetic field. The first two require a feedback network in order to be self-running.

The third one, (as described in detail in *Science & Mechanics* magazine, Spring,1980), requires critical sizes, shapes, orientations, and spacings of magnets, but no feedback. Such a motor could drive an electric generator or reversible heat pump in one's home, year round, for free. [Complete descriptive copies of U.S. patents are $3.00 each from the U.S. Patent Office, 2021 Jefferson Davis Hwy., Arlington, VA22202; correct 7-digit patent number required.]

According to Oliver Nichelson, who has made extensive studies of Tesla and free energy machines, the device that, at first, seems to best fit Tesla's claims is found in his patent for an "Apparatus for the Utilization of Radiant Energy" Number 685,957,that was filed for on March 21, 1901 and granted on November 5, 1901.

The concept behind the older technical language is simple – an insulated metal plate is put as high as possible into the air. Another metal plate is put into the ground. A wire is run from the metal plate to one side of a capacitor and a second wire goes from the ground plate to the other side of the capacitor.

The sun, as well as other sources of radiant energy, throw off minute particles of matter positively electrified, which, impinging upon [the upper] plate, communicate continuously an electrical charge to the same. The opposite terminal of the condenser being connected to ground, which may be considered as a vast reservoir of negative electricity, a feeble current flows continuously into the condenser and inasmuch as the particles are charged to a very high potential, this charging of the condenser can continue almost indefinitely, even to the point of rupturing the dielectric.

Today, we would call this device a solar-electric panel. Tesla's invention is very different though, but the closest thing to it in conventional technology is in photovoltaics. One radical difference is that conventional solar-electric panels consist of a substrate coated with crystalline silicon; the latest use amorphous silicon.

Conventional solar panels are expensive, and, whatever the coating, they are manufactured by esoteric processes. But Tesla's solar panel is just a shiny metal plate with a transparent coating of an insulating material.

Stick one of these antenna-like panels up in the air, the higher the better, and wire it to one side of a capacitor, the other going to a good earth ground. Now the

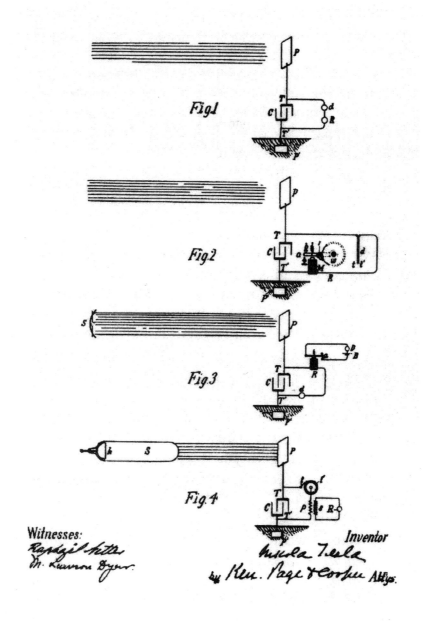

**"Apparatus for the Utilization of Radiant Energy" Patent #685,957, filed on March 21, 1901 and granted on November 5, 1901.**

energy from the sun is charging that capacitor. Connect across the capacitor some sort of switching device so that it can be discharged at rhythmic intervals, and you have an electric output.

Tesla's patent tells us that it is very simple to get electric energy. The bigger the area of the insulated plate, the more energy you get. However, this is more than a solar panel because it does not necessarily need sunshine to operate. It also produces power at night.

Of course, this is impossible according to official science. For this reason, you could not get a patent on such an invention today. Tesla's free energy receiver refers to the sun, as well as other sources of radiant energy, like cosmic rays.

That the device works at night is explained in terms of the night time availability of cosmic rays. Tesla also refers to the ground as a vast reservoir of negative electricity.

Tesla was fascinated by radiant energy and its free energy possibilities. He called the Crooke's radiometer (a device which has vanes that spin in a vacuum when exposed to radiant energy) a beautiful invention. He believed that it would become possible to harness energy directly by connecting to the very wheelwork of nature.

This seems like a very straightforward design and would seem to fulfill his claim for having developed a fuel-less generator powered by cosmic rays, but in 1900 Tesla wrote what he considered his most important article in which he describes a self-activating machine that would draw power from the ambient medium, a fuel less generator, that is different from his Radiant Energy Device.

Entitled: *The Problem of Increasing Human Energy - Through the Use of the Sun*, the article was published by his friend Robert Johnson in *The Century Illustrated Monthly* Magazine for June 1900.

The title of the chapter where he discusses this device is called: *A Departure From Known Methods – Possibility of a "Self Acting" Engine or Machine, Inanimate, Yet Capable, Like an Living Being, of Deriving Energy From the Medium – The Ideal Way of Obtaining Motive Power.*

Tesla stated he first started thinking about the idea when he read a statement by Lord Kelvin who said it was impossible to build a mechanism capable of abstracting heat from the surrounding medium and to operate by that heat. Tesla envisioned a very long bundle of metal rods, extending from the earth to outer space.

# The Lost Journals of Nikola Tesla

The earth is warmer than outer space so heat would be conducted up the bars along with an electric current. Then, all that would be needed is a very long power cord to connect the two ends of the metal bars to a motor.

The motor would continue running until the earth was cooled to the temperature of outer space. Of course, now we wouldn't need a power cord to connect the two ends – microwaves would serve.

This would be an inanimate engine which, to all evidence, would be cooling a portion of the medium below the temperature of the surrounding, and operating by the heat abstracted, that is, it would produce energy directly from the environment without the consumption of any material.

Tesla goes on in the article to describe how he worked on the development of such an energy device – here it takes a bit of detective work to focus on which of his inventions he meant.

He wrote that he first started thinking about deriving energy directly from the environment when he was in Paris during 1883, but that he was unable to do much with the idea for several years due to the commercial introduction of his alternating current generators and motors. It was not until 1889 when he again took up the idea of the self-acting machine.

In 1893, Tesla applied for a patent on an electrical coil that is the most likely candidate for a non-mechanical successor of his energy extractor. This is his "Coil for Electro-magnets," patent #512,340. It is a curious design, unlike an ordinary coil made by turning wire on a tube form, this one uses two wires laid next to each other on a form but with the end of the first one connected to the beginning of the second one.

In the patent Tesla explains that this double coil will store many times the energy of a conventional coil. The patent, however, gives no hint of what might have been its more unusual capability.

In an article for *Century Magazine*, Tesla compares extracting energy from the environment to the work of other scientists who were, at that time, learning to condense atmospheric gases into liquids. In particular he cited the work of a Dr. Karl Linde who had discovered what Tesla described as a self-cooling method for liquefying air.

As Tesla said, "This was the only experimental proof which I was still wanting that energy was obtainable from the medium in the manner contemplated by me." What ties the Linde work with Tesla's electromagnet coil is that both of them used a double path for the material they were working with. Linde had a compressor to pump the air to a high pressure, let the pressure fall as it traveled through a tube, and then used that cooled air to reduce the temperature of the incoming air by having it travel back up the first tube through a second tube enclosing the first.

The already cooled air added to the cooling process of the machine and quickly condensed the gases to a liquid. Tesla's intent was to condense the energy trapped between the earth and its upper atmosphere and to turn it into an electric current.

He pictured the sun as an immense ball of electricity, positively charged with a potential of some 200 billion volts. The Earth, on the other hand, is charged with negative electricity.

The tremendous electrical force between these two bodies constituted, at least in part, what he called cosmic energy. It varied from night to day and from season to season but it is always present.

Tesla's patents for electrical generators and motors were granted in the late 1880's. During the 1890's the large electric power industry, in the form of Westinghouse and General Electric, came into being. With tens of millions of dollars invested in plants and equipment, the industry was not about to abandon a very profitable ten year old technology for yet another new one.

Tesla saw that profits could be made from the self-acting generator, but somewhere along the line it was pointed out to him the negative impact the device would have on the newly emerging technological revolution of the late 19th and early 20th centuries.

At the end of his article in *Century* he wrote: "I worked for a long time fully convinced that the practical realization of the method of obtaining energy from the sun would be of incalculable industrial value, but the continued study of the subject revealed the fact that while it will be commercially profitable if my expectations are well founded, it will not be so to an extraordinary degree."

Years later, in 1933, he was more pointed in his remarks about the introduction of his fuel-less generator. In the *Philadelphia Public Ledger* of November 2, is an interview with Tesla under the headline: *Tesla 'Harnesses' Cosmic Energy.*

In it he was asked whether the sudden introduction of his principle would upset the present economic system, Dr. Tesla replied, "It is badly upset already." He added: "Now as never before was the time ripe for the development of new resources." At a press conference to celebrate his 76th birthday, Tesla announced that he had invented a cosmic-ray motor.

# The Lost Journals of Nikola Tesla

When asked if it was more powerful than the Crooke's radiometer, he answered, "Thousands of times more powerful." Tesla claimed that from the electric potential that exists between the elevated plate(plus) and the ground (minus), energy builds in the capacitor, and, after a suitable time interval, the accumulated energy will manifest itself in a powerful discharge.

Unfortunately, this invention, like so many others that Tesla claimed near the end of his life, allegedly never was developed. At least it was never developed publicly. When he died, there were in all, the approximate equivalent of a railroad boxcar load of Tesla materials confiscated by the government, from around four different storage locations.

Of this, a total of only about 150,000 documents were released to Tesla's Yugoslavian relatives, now held by the Tesla Institute in Belgrade. These documents and old models, primarily of a historical nature, comprise most of the published Tesla materials of the institute.

A huge volume of documents and models were retained by the Custodian of Alien Properties in an unclassified state, because the government's experts had declared that none of it was worth classifying.

From 1943 until 1945, when, following the arrival of the Nazi scientists and the secret war files of Nazi Germany, acquired under Operation Paperclip, officials from Wright-Patterson Air Force Base hurried up to the warehouses of the Custodian of Alien Properties, and took possession of all the documents and other materials, all which were classified at the highest level.

The remainder of Tesla's papers in government hands are still classified. There are literally tons of notes, documents, drawings, and plans, as well as the over twenty boxes of still missing Tesla material. The government distributed false rumors that Tesla never kept notes, which was a blatant lie.

To this day, there is no way of knowing whether or not Tesla's cosmic ray motor was practical or not. However, evidence found in Tesla's lost journals seems to indicate that free energy is possible and within the framework of known science.

Richard (Scott) McKie designed and tested in 1991 a small model of a Power On Demand MODule. The circuitry invokes Tesla's theories of electron flow, resonance, and magnetism, combined with modern theories on high frequency electronics and radio antennas to generate power directly, without the inefficient conversion of energy from other sources.

Tesla applied the knowledge gained from his Colorado experiments in the construction of Wardenclyffe in what is today Shoreham, Long Island. This facility was to be his crowning achievement: a World Telegraphy Center. Tesla envisioned not only the broadcast of news and transmission of encoded personal messages, but also a universal time code and the transmission of electricity.

# The Lost Journals of Nikola Tesla

## Free Energy Research Today

Patrick G. Bailey, Ph. D. in his *Review Of Zero Point Energy And Free Energy Theory, Progress, And Devices* – writes that the study of the free energy field overlaps with quite a number of other areas of science and technology that are not well understood, and are usually called "fringe areas."

Bailey believes that responsible investigations in these areas do uncover important information and data that can relate to various questions that occur in the study of free energy.

These questions include: Why is this research not conducted? Is it suppressed? Why is it suppressed? Are there other examples of such suppression? Where can I get more information? Are there any examples of such advanced related technologies? If such energy sources exist, has anyone found out how to use them? How do they work? Can I use them, and can I use them in a responsible manner?

There is a great outcry by those familiar with our current energy policy and the public electricity utility network for need of a new breakthrough in the technology of energy production. Dr. Gary Johnson, a college professor and IEEE Senior Member, recently published a short review of the researchers in this area in a noted US technical journal and concluded his four page report with the statement:

"There is a great deal of noise in the literature. Some concepts are obviously nonsense. Others will prove to be in error. But is there any signal in all the noise? There is if Tesla, Moray, and Bearden are correct. The potential payoff is enormous, so the search should be continued if there is any chance at all of success."

Also, Llewellen King, publisher of *The Energy Daily*, *Defense Week*, and *Environmental Week* newsletters in Washington DC recently strongly and dramatically stated in a speech to an international technical conference:

"We have failed with energy to come up with the 'Great Big Breakthrough!' 'The Major Change.' 'The Radically Different Thing.' 'The Quantum Leap Forward.' Where is the jump from a copper wire to a fiber or to a cable? Where is the equivalent of fiber optics for electricity? ... The new technologies such as magnetohydrodynamics, (are advancing and coming forth), and yet these things have not fostered – and we are still boiling water! It is theoretically possible that we could at some point take this 'Quantum Leap Forward.' And in order to do that, I believe that you will need new institutions to deploy new technology.

"They won't be deployed by the extant of the old institutions. The challenge in technology is to find It, and then sell It, and finally to deploy It."

Does there exist a conspiracy to suppress free energy devices – like the suppression that confronted Tesla with his free-energy receiver? There is the possibility that there is a collection and network of vested interest groups that seem to tightly band together for mutual financial survival.

The actions taken by any of these groups may be completely independent from the others. As well, some sort of control and suppression in the press seems very evident. Ken MacNeill published in 1983 a very disturbing article entitled "Insights into the Proprietary Syndrome," in which he points out that over 3,000 patents have been suppressed!

Two historical events are worth including here regarding possible suppression and inability to commercialize free energy devices. These are the Over-Unity Device of T. Henry Moray, and the Hindershot Motor. Both of these devices were publicly demonstrated to the US press in the 1930s, and carefully conducted tests were made to assess these devices.

From the newspaper reports and clippings, it appears that both devices passed all tests, only to fall into oblivion. What exactly happened to the devices, their inventors, and the technology is not known. It also appears that the secrets of the devices died with their inventors.

Toby Grotz has presented theory and results of Project Tesla to determine if the earth's electrostatic (atmospheric) Schumann Cavity can be resonated, if the power that is delivered to the cavity propagates with very low losses, and if power can be extracted at other locations within the cavity. A theoretical analysis of Tesla's "Death Ray" was also presented by Toby Grotz (1991).

By carefully examining historical records, this 1937 design was probably the first attempt to construct a high voltage particle beam device. Tesla's estimates indicate that a five meter diameter metal sphere charged to 60 million volts could project a high energy charged particle beam up to 60 kilometers through the air in a given direction.

In 1991, Oliver Nichelson summarized two of Tesla's later energy generation device designs, including a turbine-shaped Unipolar Dynamo design for a machine that can continue to produce electricity after being disconnected from an outside power source. This paper is also important because it also describes Tesla's "Coil for Electro-Magnetics," patented in 1893.

# *The Lost Journals of Nikola Tesla*

## Following in Tesla's Footprints

In the early 1900's, Dr. T. Henry Moray of Salt Lake City produced his first device to tap energy from the metafrequency oscillations of empty space itself. Eventually Moray was able to produce a free energy device weighing sixty pounds and producing 50,000 watts of electricity for several hours. Ironically, although he demonstrated his device repeatedly to scientists and engineers, Moray was unable to obtain funding to develop the device further into a useable power station that would furnish electrical power on a mass scale. Like Tesla, Moray had run afoul of those who had an "energy monopoly" and were not willing to share.

As a boy, Moray had been deeply inspired by Nikola Tesla. Moray was especially enthusiastic by Tesla's claims of free energy, and his emphasis on frequencies as the stuff of the universe. When Moray finished high school he went abroad to study, and took resident examinations for his doctorate in electrical engineering from the University of Uppsala, Sweden, during the period 1912-14.

Moray at first theorized that energy was coming from within the earth. Through continuous experimentation and in spite of the doubts held by the scientific community of the day, he discovered that the energy was not coming from the ground but from an outside source away from the earth.

The energy came in continuous surges, like waves of the sea, more in the daytime than at night. At this time Moray had enough power to light a 16-candle power carbon lamp at about one-half capacity. He labeled and defined his "Radiant Energy: the source of energy coming from the cosmos to the earth and radiating back from whence it came."

Around 1920, Moray produced his first elementary device that delivered measurable electrical power, and he continued to work diligently on energy devices when he had time. In the 1920's and 1930's he steadily improved his devices, particularly his detector tube, the only real secret of the device according to Moray himself.

In his book, *The Sea Of Energy In Which The Earth Floats*, Moray presents documented evidence that he invented the first transistor-type valve in 1925. In his free energy detector tube Moray apparently used, inside the tube itself, a variation of this transistor idea—a small rounded pellet of a mixture of triboluminescent zinc, a semiconductor material, and a radioactive material.

# The Lost Journals of Nikola Tesla

Channeling the waves of energy was done by way of an antenna. When set up and connected to the ground, priming and then tuning, the device would draw electrical energy. Results of this experimentation proved that the power generation had not originated from within the device. The device, through channeling radiant energy, produced up to 50,000 Watts of power and worked for long periods of time.

According to John Moray, highly energetic cosmic rays from space are tapped by the machine, which is in subharmonic resonance with this high-frequency energy level, and it converts this energy level into a usable form of electricity. However, John Moray's use of the term "cosmic ray" is not necessarily the same as that of modern physics, but in fact is the same as the present concept of zero-point energy of vacuum.

Moray envisioned all space filled with tremendously high frequency vibrations carrying vast and incalculable amounts of pure raw energy. He envisioned the dynamic Universe as a turbulent source of great energy, just as the ocean waves carry energy throughout the earth. This idea was also shared by Tesla,

Moray's patent application (never granted) was filed on July 13, 1931, long before the advent of the Bell Laboratories' transistor. Moray successfully demonstrated his radiant energy device to electrical engineering professors, congressmen, dignitaries, and a host of other visitors to his laboratory. Moray even moved his device several miles out in the country, away from all power lines, to prove that he was not simply tuning in to energy being clandestinely radiated from some other part of his laboratory.

Several times he allowed independent investigators to completely disassemble his device and reassemble it, then reactivate it themselves. In all tests, he was successful in demonstrating that the device could produce energy output without any appreciable energy input. According to exhaustive documentation, no one was ever able to prove that the device was fraudulent or that Moray had not accomplished exactly what he claimed.

On the other hand, the records are full of signed statements from physicists, electrical engineers, and scientists who came to the Moray laboratory as skeptics and left convinced that Moray had succeeded in tapping a universal source of energy that could produce free electrical power.

But despite his successes, the U.S. Patent Office refused to grant Moray a patent, first, because his device used a cold cathode in the tubes (the patent examiner asserted it was common knowledge that a heated cathode was necessary to obtain electrons) and, second, because he failed to identify the source of the energy.

All sorts of irrelevant patents and devices were also presented as being infringed upon or duplicated by Moray's work. Each of these objections was patiently answered and nullified by Moray; nonetheless, the patent has still not been issued to this day, although Moray's family still keep the patent application current.

According to writer Tom Bearden, one of Moray's efforts to develop the machine involved an association with the Rural Electrification Agency for a short time before World War II. At that time, the R.E.A. was apparently infiltrated at the highest levels by Communist sympathizers. These officials continually urged Moray to turn over all details of his device to the Soviet Union, and even arranged the visit of high level Soviet scientists to the Moray laboratory to see the device in operation.

It is thought that because of Moray's dealings with the R.E.A. – much of his important work was obtained clandestinely by the Soviet Union. Bearden speculates that Moray's work inspired the Soviets to develop the hyperspace amplifiers later used in their psychotronic weapons.

Moray became quite alarmed at the continued attempts of his R.E.A. contacts to get the device into the hands of the Russians. He eventually concluded that he had become involved with a governmental group filled with radicals and reactionaries. Much like Tesla, Moray became concerned that fifth column activity was actually directed against him in an attempt to steal his device.

Perhaps because of his misgivings, Moray was wounded by a gunshot in his own laboratory on March 2, 1940. No details have ever surfaced concerning who fired the shot or if Moray was the intended target. Moray finally discontinued his association with the R.E.A. in February 1941.

Unfortunately, Moray's basic unit was destroyed in 1939 by a man who had wanted Moray to fully disclose the inner workings and construction of his device. In Moray's day there was no theory predicting that empty space contained prodigious quantities of energy. Modern followers of quantum geometrodynamics assert the truth of Tesla's original vision. Today we know that one cubic centimeter of pure vacuum contains enough energy to condense into $1080 - 10120$ grams of matter. Thus the major part of Tesla's and Moray's thesis – that vacuum itself contains unlimited energy – is vindicated today.

# The Lost Journals of Nikola Tesla

## The Mystery of the Tesla Electric Car

With the high price of gasoline and the ever growing concern for our environment, the concept of an all electric car is once again being considered by the major auto manufacturers. Unfortunately, the problem with battery weight and storage still makes electric cars economically unfeasible.

In an article by Arthur Abrom for the *Dallas Morning News*, it was pointed out that electric powered automobiles were one of the earliest considerations and this mode of propulsion enjoyed a brief but short reign. In the early days of automobile development, electric propulsion was considered and used.

An electric powered automobile possessed many advantages that the noisy, cantankerous, smoke-belching gasoline cars could not offer. First and foremost is the absolute silence one experiences when riding in an electrically powered vehicle. There is not even a hint of noise.

One simply turns a key and steps on the accelerator - the vehicle moves instantly. No cranking from the start, no crank to turn (this was before electric starters), no pumping of the accelerator, no spark control to advance and no throttle linkage to pre-set before starting. One simply turned the ignition switch to on and away you went.

If one wants to increase speed, you simply depress the accelerator, further there is never any hesitation. Releasing the accelerator causes the vehicle to slow down immediately – you are always in complete control. It is not difficult to understand why these vehicles were so very popular around the turn of the century and until around 1915.

The big disadvantage to these cars then, and even today, was their range and need for recharging every night. All of these electric vehicles used a series of batteries and a D.C. motor. The batteries require constant recharging and the range of travel was restricted to about 100 miles. Many of the large department stores in metropolitan areas began purchasing delivery trucks that were electrically powered. They were silent and emitted no pollutants. They were almost the perfect car.

Maintenance was a minimum on electrically powered vehicles. There were few mechanics and garages in operation in the early 1900's. So city life and travel appeared to be willing to embrace the electric automobile.

Two things happened to dampen the popularity of the electric automobile. One was the subconscious craving for speed that gripped all auto enthusiasts of this era. Electric vehicles could not reach speeds of 45 or 50 m.p.h. for this would have destroyed the batteries in moments. Bursts of speeds of 25 to 35 m.p.h. could be maintained for a moment or so.

Normal driving speed, depending upon traffic conditions, was 15 to 20 m.p.h. by 1900 to 1910 standards, this was an acceptable speed limit to obtain from your electric vehicle. As well, the electric automobile could not be adapted to accommodate and utilize Tesla's polyphase A.C. motor. So, somewhere around 1915 or so, the electric automobile became just a memory.

In 1931, under the financing of Pierce-Arrow and George Westinghouse, a 1931 Pierce-Arrow was selected to be tested at the factory grounds in Buffalo, N.Y. The standard internal combustion engine was removed and an 80-H.P. 1800 r.p.m electric motor installed to the clutch and transmission. The A.C. motor measured 40 inches long and 30 inches in diameter and the power leads were left standing in the air – no external power source.

At the appointed time, Nikola Tesla arrived from New York City and inspected the Pierce-Arrow automobile. He then went to a local radio store and purchased a handful of tubes, wires and assorted resistors. A box measuring 24 inches long, 12 inches wide and 6 inches high was assembled housing the circuit.

The box was then placed on the front seat and had its wires connected to the air cooled, brushless motor. Two rods 1/4" in diameter stuck out of the box about 3" in length. Mr. Tesla got into the driver's seat, pushed the two rods in and stated, "We now have power." He put the car into gear and it moved forward.

This vehicle, powered by an A.C. motor, was driven to speeds of 90 m.p.h. and performed better than any internal combustion engine of its day. One week was spent testing the vehicle. Several newspapers in Buffalo reported this test.

When asked where the power came from, Tesla replied, "From the ethers all around us." Several people suggested that Tesla was mad and somehow in league with sinister forces of the universe. He became incensed, removed his mysterious box from the vehicle and returned to his laboratory in New York City.

His secret apparently died with him. It is speculated that Tesla was able to somehow harness the earth's magnetic field that encompasses our planet. And, he somehow was able to draw tremendous amounts of power by cutting these lines of force or causing them to be multiplied together. The exact nature of his device remains a mystery.

# The Lost Journals of Nikola Tesla

In 1969, Joseph R. Zubris took his 1961 Mercury and pulled out the Detroit internal combustion engine. He then installed an electric motor as a source of power. His unique wiring system cut the energy drain at starting to 75% of normal and doubled the electrical efficiency of the electric motor when operating.

The U.S. Patent Office issued him a patent No. 3,809,978. Although he approached many concerns for marketing, no one really seemed to be interested. And, his unique system is still not on the market.

In the 1970's, an inventor used an Ev-Gray generator, which intensified battery current, the voltage being induced to the field coils by a very simple programmer (sequencer). By allowing the motor to charge separate batteries as the device ran, phenomenally tiny currents were needed.

The device was tested at the Crosby Research Institute of Beverly Hills, Ca., a 10- horsepower EMA motor ran for over a week (9 days) on four standard automobile batteries. The inventors estimated that a 50-horsepower electric motor could traverse 300 miles at 50 m.p.h. before needing a re-charge.

Dr. Keith E. Kenyon, the inventor from Van Nuys, California discovered a discrepancy in the normal and long accepted laws relating to electric motor magnets. Dr. Kenyon demonstrated his invention for many scientists and engineers in 1976 but their reaction was astounding. Although admitting Dr. Kenyon's device worked, they saw little or no practical application for it.

The ultimate source for a successful electrically powered automobile would be to have an electric motor that required no outside source of power. Sounds impossible because it violates all current scientific thought. Nevertheless, it has been invented and H.R. Johnson has been issued a patent No. 4,151,431 on April 24, 1979 on such a device.

This new design although originally suggested by Tesla in 1905, is a permanent magnet motor. Mr. Johnson has arranged a series of permanent magnets on the rotor and a corresponding series – with different spacing – on the stator. One simply has to move the stator into position and rotation of the rotor begins immediately.

Johnson's patent states: "The invention is directed to the method of utilizing the unpaired electron spins in ferro-magnetic and other materials as a source of magnetic fields for producing power without any electron flow as occurs in normal conductors and to permanent magnet motors for utilization of this method to produce a power source.

# *The Lost Journals of Nikola Tesla*

In the practice of this invention, the unpaired electron spins occurring within permanent magnets are used to produce a motive power source solely through the super-conducting characteristics of a permanent magnet and the magnetic flux created by the magnets are controlled and concentrated to orient the magnetic forces generated in such a manner to do useful continuous work such as the displacement of a rotor with respect to a stator.

The timing and orientation of special magnetic forces at the rotor and stator components produced by permanent magnets to produce a motor is accomplished with the proper geometrical relationship of these components. Engineers of Hitachi Magnetics Corp. of California have stated that a motor run solely by magnets is feasible and logical but the politics of the matter make it impossible for them to pursue developing a magnet motor or any device that would compete with the energy cartels.

In fact, it appears that such devices have been deliberately suppressed over the years to prevent any competition from machines that can generate power without a fuel source. This would put big oil and other energy cartels out of business.

## The Real Reason For Tesla's Interest in Free Energy

According to Tesla's private journals, anomalous voice transmissions heard over his special radio receivers, discussed the warming of the planet caused by natural and manmade sources of atmospheric pollutants. Tesla was also left with the impression that the unknown voices favored this outcome and may have actually "hurried" the process along by encouraging the development of the internal combustion engine.

Tesla may have been the first human to learn about what is referred to today as "Global Warming" and the "Greenhouse Effect." Tesla, convinced that the voices he was receiving were from a hostile extraterrestrial source, began a concerted effort to develop a means of power that did not use the burning of wood or fossil fuels. An energy source that was clean and unlimited and would prevent pollutants, at least manmade, from filling the atmosphere and causing the retention of heat from the sun.

Tesla was the first to become aware of one of the most controversial subjects in conspiratorial circles today – Alternative Three and the destruction of earth!

# Chapter Eight
## *The Truth About Alternative 3*

Nikola Tesla became aware early in the 20<sup>th</sup> century that the planet was heating up, so much so that by the first decades of the 21<sup>st</sup> century, Earth would be almost uninhabitable for the human species. Tesla's source of information was the weird voices he was picking up off of his specially modified radio receiver.

These mysterious voice broadcasts were the outcome of Tesla's initial research into strange radio signals he picked up during his experiments at Colorado Springs in 1899. By now, Tesla had improved his receiving equipment to enable him to pickup voice broadcasts. However, these voices were being heard on frequencies that were suppose to be unable to carry these kinds of transmissions, but they were there nevertheless.

Tesla wrote that these voices were of men from other worlds – men who had lived on Earth sometime in its prehistoric past, had developed the technology to colonize nearby space and were still interested in the inhabitants they had left behind. These men had colonized the planet Mars as well as maintaining bases on the moon. Others of their kind had gone deeper into space, out of our solar system altogether to explore the galaxy.

It had been decided that the Earth was to become a reserve so to speak, to allow nature to take its course and new species to evolve and fill the niches left vacant by the departure of its first inhabitants. However, some things were not left to nature alone. The first men decided to leave behind remnants of themselves in the form of our early ancestors. Tesla's description of the re-seeding of planet Earth with intelligent hominids sounds very much like genetic manipulation.

This could explain why reports of UFO occupants, who claim extraterrestrial origins, look so much like us. The majority of contacts with beings who step out of UFOs all agree on their human-like appearance. With very few exceptions, all alleged extraterrestrials possess very human features. One head with two eyes a nose and a mouth, two arms, two hands with five fingers, two legs and feet. Many have been reported to be so human in appearance that they are indistinguishable from normal humans. Maybe this is because they are human – the first humans.

Of course, Tesla died before the modern UFO wave, but his descriptions of his purported extraterrestrials bear an uncanny resemblance to our UFO occupants.

# The Lost Journals of Nikola Tesla

## An April Fools Joke too Close to the Truth

At 9:00 PM on Monday June 20 1977, Anglia television based in Norwich United Kingdom, put out a one hour TV special. The program was to be simultaneously transmitted to a number of other countries which included Australia, New Zealand, Canada, Iceland, Norway, Sweden, Finland, Greece, and Yugoslavia. The name of the TV special was called *Alternative 3*, it was to shock the nation, jam media telephone lines and rock the station's credibility.

At 10:00 PM Anglia was besieged with calls from irate viewers demanding more information. Callers were told not to panic, the program was simply an April Fools hoax that had been pre-empted until June 20. However, many were not convinced that it was a hoax.

The following morning the *Daily Express* newspaper confirmed the program was a hoax and pointed out that Dr Carl Gerstein was none other than the well known actor Richard Marner. Meanwhile back at Anglia there were rumors of industrial action and the station was severely criticized for putting out the hoax. Anglia got a reprimand and the public were relieved of their fears.

The *Alternative 3* TV special was put together by a respectable team of reporters who had a regular weekly slot titled *Science Report.* It was an intelligent documentary series which reported on new scientific inventions. It was because of the teams' credibility that *Alternative 3* was taken so seriously. The question was: Why would a serious investigative team who had a weekly documentary slot suddenly produce a hoax?

In 1976 the United Kingdom was plagued with "The Brain Drain," a term used for the mass exodus of some of the countries best surgeons and scientists which were being enticed with huge pay checks by the United States. There were also reports of suicides and disappearances among scientists. As well, there were small communities such as "Friends of the Earth," and others who were just beginning to understand the ozone problem and global warming.

By 1978 the story took on new life when Sphere Books published *Alternative 3* by Leslie Watkins, David Ambrose and Christopher Miles. According to Watkins, Ambrose and Miles didn't help write the book, but their names were included for copyright purposes because they had written the television program on which it was based. Those who were able to get a hold of a copy, read a story that was a follow-up of the TV special produced by Spectrum for Anglia TV.

Both the book and the TV program focused on a number of amazing scenarios, all said to be factual.

■   There is a secret joint U.S./U.S.S.R. space program that has gone far beyond what the public sees. Astronauts landed on Mars in 1962. It has been discovered that there is other intelligent life in the universe and they are observing and interacting with the inhabitants of Earth. The Earth is dying due to natural and manmade pollutants. The increasing Greenhouse Effect will cause the polar ice caps and glaciers to melt and flood the Earth.

■   Extreme heat, such as that which is now inevitable, will melt land glaciers. That will result in a marked rise in sea level and then there'll be the start of the extensive flooding - with London and New York among the first cities to be affected.(*Alternative 3*)

There are three possible solutions for mankind: *Alternative 1* - Stop all pollution immediately and blow two huge holes in the ozone layer. This would allow excessive UV light to reach the earth and millions would die of skin cancer.

*Alternative 2* - Immediately begin digging underground cities for world leaders, the very rich and leaders of big business and a few selected scientists. The remainder of the population will be left to perish on the polluted surface.

*Alternative 3* - Build spaceships and get the Elite off the planet - to the moon and Mars. Kidnap and take along some "ordinary" people for use as slave labor. Use mind control techniques to control them. Leave the remainder of humanity to die on the planet.

Was the Anglia Television program fact or fiction? Reporter Georginia Bruni spoke to Christopher Miles, who also directed and co-wrote the program. Miles admitted that the program was entirely fiction, but he now suspects that they may have accidently come a little too close to the hidden truth with *Alternative 3*.

The writer of the book, Leslie Watkins, was a writer of thrillers even before *Alternative 3*. The *Fortean Times* recently printed an article in which Nick Austin, then editorial director of Sphere Books, revealed how he commissioned

Leslie Watkins to write the book version at the behest of literary agent Murray Pollinger. Watkins, in a letter to Windwords Bookstore, outlined his beliefs concerning the mystery surrounding *Alternative 3*, and how he may have accidently stumbled upon top secret truths that others wanted to be kept quiet.

"The book *Alternative 3* is based on fact, but uses that fact as a launchpad for a HIGH DIVE INTO FICTION. In answer to specific questions:
1) There is no astronaut named Grodin.
2) There is no Sceptre Television and the reported Benson is also fictional.
3) There is no Dr. Gerstein.
4) Yes, a 'documentary' was televised in June 1977 on Anglia Television, which went out to the entire national network in Britain. It was called *Alternative 3* and was written by David Ambrose and produced by Christopher Miles (whose names were on the book for contractual reasons). This original TV version, which I EXPANDED IMMENSELY for the book, was ACTUALLY A HOAX which had been scheduled for transmission on April Fools' Day. Because of certain problems in finding the right network slot, the transmission was delayed.

"The TV program did cause a tremendous uproar because viewers refused to believe it was fiction. I initially took the view that the basic premise was so way out, particularly the way I aimed to present it in the book, that no one would regard it as non-fiction. Immediately after publication, I realized I was totally wrong. In fact, the amazing mountains of letters from virtually all parts of the world, including vast numbers from highly intelligent people in positions of responsibility, convinced me that I had ACCIDENTALLY trespassed into a range of top-secret truths.

"Documentary evidence provided by many of these correspondents decided me to write a serious and COMPLETELY NON-FICTION sequel. Unfortunately, a chest containing the bulk of the letters was among the items which were mysteriously LOST IN TRANSIT some four years when I moved from London, England, to Sydney, Australia, before I moved on to settle in New Zealand.

"For some time after *Alternative 3* was originally published, I have reason to suppose that my home telephone was being tapped and my contacts who were experienced in such matters were convinced that certain intelligence agencies considered that I probably knew too much.

"So, summing up, the book is FICTION BASED ON FACT. But I now feel that I inadvertently got VERY CLOSE TO A SECRET TRUTH."

# The Lost Journals of Nikola Tesla

## None Dare Call it Alternative 3

It is amazing to consider that Nikola Tesla, sometime in the 1920's first wrote in his personal journals his thoughts concerning the buildup of greenhouse gases in the Earth's atmosphere. These gases, caused by manmade and natural pollutants were to eventually cause the planet's overall temperature to increase to such a point that the polar icecaps would melt, flooding the coastlines. As well, weather patterns would change dramatically bringing about fierce storms, droughts in some areas and floods in others. Agriculture would be destroyed and life as we know it would cease to exist.

So, while the name Alternative 3 may have been nothing more then the imagination of a clever television writer – the basic premise, that the greenhouse effect caused by air pollution would make human life on Earth extremely hazardous, is probably correct. And Nikola Tesla allegedly first came across this disturbing information while monitoring late into the night, mysterious voices on his specialized receiver.

Tesla theorized that the planet's developing pollution problems were being closely monitored by extraterrestrials who were studying Earth and its inhabitants. Tesla was indecisive on whether or not these intelligence's were hostile, friendly or indifferent. He had no clear-cut evidence that the information he had been receiving was factual – in fact, Tesla often wrote that if it were not for the unusual way that he was getting this knowledge, he would have dismissed it long ago as the ravings of a madman. Nevertheless, Tesla was intrigued enough to devote most of his later years to research and inventions based on the voice transmissions he was receiving from his Martials.

Some researchers have attributed Ronald Reagan's Space Defense Initiative to a branch of Alternative 3. This special project was using a portion of its black budget to build a space based weapon system to be deployed not against Soviet nuclear missiles, but instead, to a perceived threat against hostile extraterrestrial forces.

In *Genesis Revisited*, Zecharia Sitchin maintains that the world's leaders "...have been aware for some time, first, that there is one more planet in our solar system and, second, that we are not alone." He claims that only this knowledge can explain the incredible changes in world affairs that have been taking place with even more incredible speed.

Certainly both Reagan and Gorbachev have referred to threats from extraterrestrials. Speaking at Fallston, Maryland, on December 4, 1985, Reagan stated: "Just think how easy his (Gorbachev's) task and mine might be in these meetings that we held if suddenly there was a threat to this world from some other species from another planet outside the universe. We'd forget all the little local differences that we have between our countries and we would find out once and for all that we are all human beings here on Earth together."

On February 16, 1987, at the Grand Kremlin Palace, Moscow, Gorbachev observed: "At our meeting in Geneva, the US President said that if the Earth faced an invasion by extraterrestrials, the United States and the Soviet Union would join forces to repel such an invasion. I shall not dispute the hypothesis, though I think it's early yet to worry about such an intrusion."

In an address to the General Assembly of the United Nations on September 21, 1987, speaking of the need to turn swords into ploughshares, Reagan said: "In our obsession with antagonisms of the moment, we often forget how much unites all the members of humanity. Perhaps we need some outside, universal threat to recognize this common bond. I occasionally think how quickly our differences would vanish if we were facing an alien threat from outside this world."

The late UFO investigator Leonard Stringfield states in Timothy Good's *The UFO Report* : "Star Wars, ostensibly conceived as a defensive system against Russian missile attacks, may have had from its beginning a 'defensive' UFO connection."

Documentary evidence of such an agenda appears to have been inadvertently provided by NASA when the astronauts of the Shuttle Discovery transmitted to Earth, video camera footage of UFOs traversing just above Earth atmosphere. One UFO suddenly makes a 90-degree turn to the right and accelerates off into deeper space, just a second before a burst of shaped pulse high energy streaks up from Earth towards the spot where the UFO would have been if it had not radically changed course. Other UFOs are shown being shot at by visibly energized EM weapon bursts.

What is the motive for the undeclared war on extraterrestrials? Richard Hoagland, former editor of *Star & Sky* magazine explains: "There is a great deal of naiveté about the forces in our society that do not want this knowledge, even in the form of a very useful technology, to get out." He notes that there are "interlocking institutions whose job it is to keep themselves in business. And they do not take lightly to this ET technology. After all, how do people stay in power? Because they define the universe as limited, rare and scarce and then put a price tag on it. Then some people are put in charge of doling out the scarce precious thing; other people buy it at whatever the market will bear. And you have a really neat system for controlling people."

It is possible that the United States government (and other foreign powers) were aware of a hidden extraterrestrial presence over Earth. Tesla had confided to a few friends that he had sent a number of letters to Washington DC expressing his fear of an invasion from outer space. Tesla had also offered Washington a number of his inventions for the purpose of defending the planet against the alleged alien invaders.

Tesla was financially troubled by this time and he offered the government complete access to his research, provided that he be paid a small, monthly stipend for the use of his inventions. Tesla received no answer to his inquiries – no doubt due to the sensational nature of his letters. It was not until several years after his death that the United States military became aware of intrusions into the country's airspace by what later would be known as UFOs.

Tesla's ideas of electric death rays and particle beam weapons, while scoffed at during his lifetime, were now eagerly sought after by the military. Even though UFOs have been seen for centuries, it was not until the beginning of the 20th century that the numbers of reported encounters increased significantly. The Pentagon could think of no reason for the blatant way that UFOs were now operating except as a precursor to an invasion. The message it seemed was clear: "We can go and come as we please, and there is nothing that you can do about it."

Part of the rumors that surround Alternative 3 is the contention that the United States and Russia formed a secret partnership and constructed bases on the moon as a jumping off point for Mars. It can now be confirmed that these secret bases on the moon are real and still exist today!

Unlike the fictional TV show *Alternative 3*, the real moon bases were not installed until after Apollo 11's historic landing in 1969. Before that time, primitive remote control spacecraft containing supplies and building material had been sent to await the time when astronauts would arrive and start construction.

The remaining Apollo missions would rendevous in orbit with containers previously sent up from Vandenburg Air Force Base in California. The Apollo would then ferry the containers to the moon to be placed in orbit for later use.

# The Lost Journals of Nikola Tesla

## Someone Else is on the Moon and Mars

The Apollo moon missions served two functions, one as a public display of the United States' ability to reach the moon, the other was basically delivery of men and material to be used to construct the secret moon bases. The Apollo astronauts would not be responsible for building the first moon base – that honor would go to astronauts who would work in anonymity.

Both the United States and the former Soviet Union would participate in the construction of the moon colony. Astronauts would be sent into Earth orbit from Vandenburg and the Baikonur Space Center. Upon reaching orbit, a ferry craft would then take them the rest of the way to the moon. The first moon base was finished in 1971 and the rest were completed by 1976.

The moon has proved to be a virtual goldmine in minerals and even pockets of ice hidden in the shadows of some craters. Another exciting resource on the moon is an ample supply of the isotope helium-3, which is very rare on Earth but has been deposited on the lunar surface over billions of years by the solar wind. It is now estimated that at least a million tons of He-3 are readily recoverable from the regolith formations where lunar solar power stations would be practical. This He-3 offers a key to safe, practical nuclear fusion energy on the moon. It is estimated that a single ton of He-3 delivered to Earth would be worth at least $1 billion.

The next step was to dispatch and establish robot probes to Mars, the ultimate destination for this mission. The idea was to duplicate the successful moon colonies on Mars, with an extremely long-term goal to terraform Mars into a more hospitable planet and the new home for mankind. Unfortunately, this mission and others like it, would all end in disaster.

It was known at NASA that unusual anomalies on the surface of the moon had been seen and photographed by astronomers. In the 1920s and 1930s, American, British, and French astronomers reported glowing, moving and sometimes even blinking lights on the moon.

This interest peaked when a respected expert in aerial phenomenon, Pulitzer Prize winning astronomer John O'Neill, publicly reported observing a "bridge" on the moon that appeared artificially constructed. Many of the Gemini and Apollo astronauts have admitted that they saw UFOs while they were in orbit. Gordon Cooper has publically admitted he believes UFOs are intelligently controlled and that the government is hiding the truth.

One Soviet space mission in the 1960s, designed to set a new record for time in orbit, was mysteriously aborted right after their craft entered space. Private researchers with powerful receiving radio equipment claimed the Soviet cosmonauts were followed into orbit by UFOs, which surrounded them and began bouncing them back and forth as if they were playing a ball game with the Soviet craft. The cosmonauts reportedly panicked and reentered the Earth's atmosphere at the first available moment.

During the 1950s many UFOs were reportedly tracked back to the moon by government tracking stations in secret complexes in deserts in Arizona and Nevada and inside underground mountain bases. Soviet and American spacecraft in orbit over the moon began to photograph mysterious structures on the moon which were censored by NASA for awhile, yet were obtained by scientific researchers like Fred Steckling. Many of the structures can only be seen when these photos are blown-up to a much larger size.

Further evidence of an extraterrestrial presence on the moon comes from an Air Force veteran with an Above Top Secret security clearance. Investigative reporter Alan Carmack, who was doing research for the TV show *Strange World*, was contacted by the veteran who had an amazing story to tell. Carmack agreed not to reveal the identity of his contact because of his national security oath.

"Nearly thirty years ago, my Supervising Sergeant called me aside and informed me that there was a technical problem in a highly-classified area elsewhere on the Air Base. At that time, all systems were expanding to support increased military efforts for the Viet Nam War. As a part of that, it was my job to support and maintain highly classified Intelligence and Reconnaissance related Electronic Photographic Systems, recently installed in a new Top Secret facility on the Base. Our unit was under the command of the Director of Intelligence at Headquarters SAC, Tactical Air Command, Langley Field, Virginia.

"My Supervisor stated that the Lunar Orbiter program had encountered a problem with an Electronic Photographic Contact Printer, identical to equipment that was utilized in the darkrooms of our own Unit. This was the first Lunar Orbiter program, the purpose of which was to bring back the first close-up pictures of the surface of the moon. These photos would later be utilized to select an appropriate landing site for the first manned landing on the moon, in 1969.

"As the only Electronics Repairman on the Base with a Cryptologic Security Clearance, a step above Top Secret, I was being loaned to the project to see if I could resolve the system problem. More than excited at the prospect of helping out and possibly having a chance to view the first close up photos of the surface of the moon, I was briefed on security, and gathered the appropriate equipment and tools for the task.

"Driving across the Base on the perimeter access road that skirted the flat dusty fields and long runways in the distance, I noticed an experimental helicopter hovering fly-like in the air just above and to the south of the massive arching metal-grey hanger, one of the largest on the base that housed the Lunar Orbiter project.

"Upon entering the hanger, I was asked to present my Top Secret Identity Badge, in exchange for their internal higher-level Identity Badge; this was to be worn around the neck on a chain. Another guard escorted me through a series of security doors to an expansive open area within the hanger.

"Large black fabric curtains hung from a metal grid suspended from the ceiling. These, in effect, cordoned off various working areas within the larger space. Passing through one of the draped areas, I entered a large open space where people in small groups stood talking quietly, with a sense of seriousness and concern.

"I was immediately struck by the number of people who were present, who appeared to be civilians, and also some scientists from other countries. With a bit of instant shock and judgement, I thought to my self, why are they here? I had a very strange feeling - a feeling that something is off here, something is not quite right.

"I was introduced to a man dressed in civilian clothes and a lab coat, the head of the project, a Dr. Collie, I believe. In a very gracious and reserved manner, bringing to mind an image of Sherlock Holmes, he softly conveyed to me that the equipment in question was holding up the processing of the first close-up photographs of the surface of the moon and also delaying the release of photos to be provided for study and release to the world, and how grateful the program staff would be if there was anything that I could do.

"An Airman escorted me into a darkroom. Inside, another young Airman assembled strips of high resolution 35mm film into what is called a mosaic. He was placing side-by-side successively numbered photographic scans of the lunar surface, which had been transmitted back to earth from the Lunar Orbiter. Each surface scan covered a narrow band of terrain, and successive orbits around the moon were required to assemble a complete photographic image of the lunar terrain.

"The mosaic negative created by that process was then placed into a Resolution Enhancing Contact Printer. Photographic paper was placed on top of the negative, and an exposure begun. The negative was scanned by an electron light beam generated by a large Cathode Ray Tube, similar to the tube in a black and white televison set.

"The light beam was picked up by a photo-multiplier tube and, through a feedback loop, modulated by the various changes in density of the photographic negative, enhancing the contrast, brightness and resolution of the image in the process. The resulting 9.5 inch by 18 inch high resolution contact print was then examined by a photographic interpreter or scientist, who viewed the images under a microscopic type viewer, analyzing the features and terrain of the lunar landscape.

"Left alone in the faint red light of the darkroom with the Airman and equipment, much of which I had never seen before, I began to question the technician, attempting to discern what the problem might be with the ailing contact printer. After a few minutes of investigation, it was clear that there was a problem with the electronic control circuitry, which was comprised of several small plug-in circuit modules.

"Having no spare parts on hand, it was clear that I would have to trouble-shoot each module on a component-by-component basis, a very tedious and time consuming process at best. This was something that could not be done in the faint red light of a darkroom. The unit would have to be removed from the darkroom and taken into a more appropriate space to allow for the accomplishment of the task.

"Talking with the Airman on the other side of the room, questions floated into my head. I was curious and fascinated with the whole process. How were the signals from the Lunar Orbiter transmitted to the lab? How where they converted into images on photographic film? How were the images correlated and aligned into the final mosaic negative?

"I knew these were all questions that I should not ask, in fact I could receive severe punishment for asking such questions. Yet, at the same time, I was alone with an Airman who was obviously as enthusiastic as I was about his job. I hesitated for a moment, weighing in my mind what I should do.

126

"Under normal operating conditions, many other people would have been in the lab, part of the assembly line of production. But, here we were all alone, so I began to ask all those questions.

"After about thirty minutes of technical discussion and a complete rundown on all the steps in the process, the Airman turned to me and said candidly, 'You know they've discovered a base on the back side of the moon!.' I said, 'What do you mean?,' and again he said, 'They have discovered a base on the moon!' and, surreptitiously, at the same time dropped a photograph in front of me.

"There it was, a mosaic print of the surface of the moon, with some sort of geometric structures clearly visible. Scrutinizing the image, I could see spheres and towers. My first thought was, 'Whose base is it?' Then I realized the full implication: it was not anyone of this earth.

"I didn't dwell on the photograph - I quickly took it in visually and moved away in case someone else should enter the lab. I knew that I had been given a gift, information that I should not have seen. With my position being that of a dutiful Airman, I asked no further questions and went about my business, quietly thinking to myself that I couldn't wait to hear about this on the news in the next few days! I told myself, do whatever you can to get this thing fixed...so the world can see this and hear about it!

"Two days of labors paid off – a tiny diode on one of the circuit cards had shorted. Replacing the defective component, I was as surprised as anyone that I had found the problem. Dr. Collie was more than pleased and offered several of the first photographs of the lunar surface to me in appreciation of my efforts. As he autographed some of the prints for me, I longed to ask more questions about the moon base, but knew that was forbidden, and that I would have to wait for the evening news for the answers, along with the rest of the world.

"Now, here it is more than thirty years later, and I am still waiting to hear the report on the evening news of what was found on the back side of the moon."

It has been reported that the clandestine moon bases are operated by joint teams comprising mostly scientists and technicians from the United States and Russia. There are also teams from Great Britain, Canada, France and Australia. The men who operate these secret bases are also well aware that they aren't the only ones on the moon. There are also bases apparently maintained by extraterrestrials that appear and disappear so frequently that there is no way to investigate them. These structures are located almost entirely on the opposite side of the moon.

# The Lost Journals of Nikola Tesla

## The Failure of Alternative 3

The main goal of the manned moon bases was to act as a jump point for missions to Mars. These missions, using first robotic spacecraft and then manned, were to establish a human presence on Mars with the eventual purpose of building permanent colonies.

The thinking was that with Earth soon to become extremely inhospitable to civilization, Mars would act as sort of a "foster" world for human civilization to continue to flourish. It was hoped that Earth's greenhouse effect would stabilize after about two thousand years, then the Martian colonies, with their superior technology still intact, could move back to Earth and reestablish the population.

What was not considered by the Alternative 3 planners was that there was already an intelligent presence on Mars that would not look very favorably upon interlopers from Earth.

The earliest robot probes to Mars in the 1960's ran into little trouble with the exception of mechanical problems due to the primitive electronics used at the time. The first craft to set down successfully on Mars in 1963 (Lowell III) sent back a few blurred photos showing that Mars had little atmosphere or water. Stories that now surround the Alternative 3 legend state that the secret spacecraft from the Pentagon landed on Mars in 1962 and sent back videotaped images of the surface. The video allegedly showed a Martian landscape that had canals, lakes, green vegetation, swamps, and animal life on the surface. This is a good example of the disinformation that exists to hide the actual program that the TV program *Alternative 3* was based on.

After this initial success though, further surveys of Mars ran into mysterious problems that could not be attributed to mechanical failure. The same problems were also being experienced by NASA and the Soviets who were unaware of the Alternative 3 efforts underway at the same time.

What is still not clearly understood is why some Mars missions, like the Vikings I and II landings on Mars were successful, while others ended in disaster. The first manned landing on Mars was scheduled for 1978, but it was halted when the ship being constructed in orbit around the moon was mysteriously destroyed.

Due to these unexplained failures, the Mars colonization project, which had a deadline of 1980 for its first phase, was pushed back to 1985 and finally to 1990. The entire colonization mission to Mars was finally abandoned in 1992.

Even though the TV show was declared a hoax, Leslie Watkins, author of the book, feels that certain aspects of Alternative 3, such as secret moon bases, are probably true.

# Chapter Nine
## *HAARP – Chemtrails – Alternative 4*

With the failure of Alternative 3, it became necessary to implement a new system to protect mankind from the upcoming disaster from global warming. The Mars Projects had eaten away at the combined American and Soviet budgets for Alternative 3, and now world politics would interfere at the expense of its citizens.

President Ronald Reagan who felt that destroying the "Evil Empire" was more important than fighting global warming, earmarked the remaining money from the Mars Projects for building new weapons to destroy the Soviet Union. The Soviets protested by withdrawing their cooperation for Alternative 3 and shortly thereafter collapsed as a world power. This marked the official demise of Alternative 3.

Earlier studies had estimated that the planet's temperature would rise high enough to cause the melting of the ice caps by the year 2000. Efforts to cut back air pollution in the 1970's apparently slowed down the heating to a small degree. Enough to gain about twenty extra years before disaster struck.

Unfortunately, no one had foreseen the damage to the ozone layer caused by unlimited use of fluorocarbons. A massive "hole" in the ozone layer opened up over both poles causing huge amounts of cosmic radiation to flood the planet, further aggravating the existing problem. Something had to be done and done fast, or the planet would bake from solar radiations.

It was clear that an outside intelligence had declared Mars "off limits" for human colonization. The reasons why could only be speculated, but Tesla had said years earlier that he thought Mars was inhabited both by people originally from ancient Earth and extraterrestrials from outside our solar system. He may have been right.

With the budget slashed, and Russia no longer a partner, it was now mainly up to the United States and their allies to come up with some kind of solution to the impending threat. That solution came from secret papers and letters by Tesla.

Perhaps in response to the anomalous radio signals he was receiving, Nikola Tesla said, in June, 1900, "The time is very near when we shall have the precipitation of the moisture of the atmosphere under complete control..." Tesla must have known at this point what was in store for planet Earth in the near future.

Tesla's original warnings had also caught the interest of those hastily trying to develop the successor to Alternative 3. Now that fleeing the planet is no longer an option, those in power are stuck on Earth with the rest of humanity. The only viable method now seemed to be to try and modify the weather using technology invented by Tesla years earlier.

Tesla, heeding the strange voices he heard over his modified radio receiver, started experiments to see if it was possible to change the weather using massive amounts of electrical power. There is a global circuit, sometimes referred to as the Wilson circuit, in which the ionosphere is maintained at a positive potential, generally in the range 200 to 300 kilovolts, relative to the earth.

In the non-thunderstorm (fair-weather) portions of the atmosphere, a return conduction current flows between the ionosphere and the earth, and the circuit is completed between the conducting earth and the bases of thunderclouds through a combination of conduction, convection, lightning, point discharge and precipitation currents. The charge, put on the earth by thunderstorms, maintains the earth's electric field and the ionospheric potential.

This natural global circuit, was originally discovered by Tesla in the 1890's and he once again took up research on the subject after he became convinced that the warming of the planet was being helped along by extraterrestrial forces.

The Tesla system involves using giant magnifying transmitters to act as global generators and artificially create the same global electromagnetic circuit functions that are naturally created by thunderstorm activity. Oddly enough, the first use of Tesla's idea came from the good ol' days of the Cold War and the Soviets experiments with weather modification.

On the Fourth of July, 1976, the former Soviet Union began broadcasting huge, pulsed electromagnetic fields from three gigantic 40-million watt transmitters which beamed those signals halfway around the world to the U.S. This electronic assault disrupted and jammed radio and television broadcast signals, enraged the FCC, and irritated ham radio operators, who quickly dubbed the signals "The Russian Woodpecker," because of their pulsed cadence. Originally designed to bring more rain to certain areas of Siberia, the Soviets were surprised to find that the signals also disrupted weather over North America.

The Russians completed nearly 30 of the huge transmitters which emit signals primarily in the very dangerous 10-Hertz range, otherwise known as Extreme Low Frequency (ELF). The technology was rumored to be based on the work of

Tesla. These Tesla transmitters create massive "standing" ELF waves that form major high pressure blocking systems that change the normal high altitude jet stream pattern, force it to the north, and actually retard the normal flow patterns of incoming weather systems.

As far back as April, 1969, *Spectrum*, a publication of the prestigious Institute of Electrical and Electronics Engineers, featured an article by Seymour Tilson which stated: "Workers in the field of atmospheric electricity and cloud physics have accumulated sufficient evidence to suggest that electric fields in the Earth's lower atmosphere play a critical role...perhaps the critical role...in the development and behavior of clouds that produces precipitation.

Mr. Tilson apparently was correct. Exactly one year after the start of the Russian Woodpecker, July 4, 1978, the U.S. Government conducted its own ELF weather experiment which created an enormous downpour of rain over six counties of northern Wisconsin. This ELF-generated storm generated winds of 157 mph and caused $50 million in damage, leveling Phillips, Wisconsin, and destroying several thousand acres of forest.

The first published alarm about Soviet weather control warfare came from Dr. Andrew Michrowski of PACE (Planetary Association for Clean Energy). In a published paper in 1978, Dr. Michrowski described how he had placed monitoring stations all across Canada and determined that "the Soviets managed to establish relatively stable and localized ELF fields (over North America) which were able to hamper or divert the jet stream flow in the Northern Hemisphere."

Several years later, Michrowski stated in a PACE Newsletter (Vol.4, #4): "ELF fields...propagate vertically to the ground, creating 'standing waves'...that can redistribute energy and momentum in (atmosphere) through cumulus convection. It has been consistently noted that variance of the (Soviet) ELF transmissions leads to a subsequent change in the route of the jet stream flow in the Northern Hemisphere within 72 hours.

The 2/81 PACE Newsletter reported that the Soviets turned off their ELF Woodpecker signal for a brief period in 1980: "During the two-week lull, the Northern Hemisphere's jet stream was normal... ...with the return of the Soviet ELF transmissions, the jet stream was deflected (again) by a persistent (high) pressure ridge extending from the Yukon to Arizona."

Spurned on by the success of the Russian Woodpecker signal, the United States secretly activated the High Active Auroral Research Project, or HAARP. Located in Gakon, Alaska, this Tesla-based U.S. Navy and Air Force ionospheric heater has been projecting tightly-focused beams of intense radio-frequency energy into the atmosphere for the past several years.

This controllable radio wave is so powerful and electromagnetically charged that it can actually lift and heat the ionosphere. Put simply, the apparatus for HAARP is a reversal of a radio telescope; antenna send out signals instead of receiving.

HAARP publicity states that the High-frequency Active Auroral Research Program is mainly an academic project with the goal of changing the ionosphere to improve communications for our own good. However, other U.S. military documents put it more clearly – HAARP aims to learn how to "exploit the ionosphere for Department of Defense purposes."

The patents described below were the package of ideas which were originally controlled by ARCO Power Technologies Incorporated (APTI), a subsidiary of Atlantic Richfield Company. APTI was the contractor that built the HAARP facility. ARCO sold this subsidiary, the patents and the second phase construction contract to E-Systems in June 1994.

E-Systems is one of the biggest intelligence contractors in the world – doing work for the CIA, defense intelligence organizations and others. $1.8 billion of their annual sales are to these organizations, with $800 million for Black Projects.

E-Systems was bought out by Raytheon, which is one of the largest defense contractors in the world. In 1994 Raytheon was listed as number forty-two on the Fortune 500 list of companies. Raytheon has thousands of patents, some of which will be valuable in the HAARP project.

The twelve original patents are the backbone of the HAARP project, and are now buried among the thousands of others held in the name of Raytheon. Bernard J. Eastlund's U.S. Patent # 4,686,605, "Method and Apparatus for Altering a Region in the Earth's Atmosphere, Ionosphere; and/or Magnetosphere," was sealed for a year under a government Secrecy Order.

The Eastlund ionospheric heater was different; the radio frequency (RF) radiation was concentrated and focused to a point in the ionosphere. This difference throws an unprecedented amount of energy into the ionosphere.

The Eastlund device would allow a concentration of one watt per cubic centimeter, compared to others only able to deliver about one millionth of one watt. This huge difference could lift and change the ionosphere in the ways necessary to create futuristic effects described in the patent. According to the patent, the work of Nikola Tesla in the early 1900's formed the basis of the research.

What would this technology be worth to ARCO, the owner of the patents? They could make enormous profits by beaming electrical power from a powerhouse in the gas fields to the consumer without wires.

For a time, HAARP researchers could not prove that this was one of the intended uses for HAARP. In April, 1995, however, other patents were found connected with a "key personnel" list for APTI. Some of these new APTI patents were indeed a wireless system for sending electrical power.

Eastlund's patent said the technology can confuse or completely disrupt airplanes' and missiles' sophisticated guidance systems. Further, this ability to spray large areas of Earth with electromagnetic waves of varying frequencies, and to control changes in those waves, makes it possible to knock out communications on land or sea as well as in the air.

The patent continues with: "Thus, this invention provides the ability to put unprecedented amounts of power in the Earth's atmosphere at strategic locations and to maintain the power injection level particularly if random pulsing is employed, in a manner far more precise and better controlled than heretofore accomplished by the prior art, particularly by detonation of nuclear devices of various yields at various altitudes.

"It is possible not only to interfere with third party communications but to take advantage of one or more such beams to carry out a communications network even though the rest of the world's communications are disrupted. Put another way, what is used to disrupt another's communications can be employed by one knowledgeable of this invention as a communication network at the same time.

"Large regions of the atmosphere could be lifted to an unexpectedly high altitude so that missiles encounter unexpected and unplanned drag forces with resultant destruction. Weather modification is possible by, for example, altering upper atmosphere wind patterns by constructing one or more plumes of atmospheric particles which will act as a lens or focusing device.

"Molecular modifications of the atmosphere can take place so that positive environmental effects can be achieved. Besides actually changing the molecular composition of an atmospheric region, a particular molecule or molecules can be chosen for increased presence."

Eastlund also notes NATO interest in modifying the weather for military advantage. In May, 1990 a NATO paper: *Modification of Tropospheric Propagation Conditions*, detailed how the atmosphere could be modified to absorb electromagnetic radiation by spraying polymers behind high-flying aircraft.

Absorbing microwaves transmitted by HAARP and other atmospheric heaters linked from Puerto Rico, Germany and Russia, these artificial mirrors could heat the air, inducing changes in the weather. U.S. Patent # 4253190 describes how a mirror made of "polyester resin" could be held aloft by the pressure exerted by electromagnetic radiation from a transmitter like HAARP.

A PhD polymer researcher who wishes to remain anonymous told researcher William Thomas that if HAARP's frequency output is matched to Earth's magnetic field, its tightly-beamed energy could be imparted to molecules "artificially introduced into this region." This highly reactive state could then "promote polymerization and the formation of new compounds," he explained.

The heat generation needed to modify the weather can be fostered by adding magnetic iron oxide powder to polymers exuded by many high-flying aircraft. Radio-frequency-absorbing polymers such as Phillips Ryton F-5 PPS are sensitive in the 1-50 MHz regime, HAARP transmits between two and 10 MHz.

HAARP's U.S. Air Force and Navy sponsors claim that their transmitter will eventually be able to produce 3.6 million watts of radio frequency power. But on page 185 of an October, 1991 "Technical Memorandum 195" outlining projected HAARP tests, there is a call by the ionospheric effects division of the U.S. Air Force Phillips Laboratory for HAARP to reach a peak power output of 100 billion watts. Commercial radio stations commonly broadcast at 50,000 watts.

Some hysterical reports state that HAARP-type technologies will be used to initiate weather manipulation, climate modification, polar ice-cap melting, ozone depletion, earthquake engineering and ocean wave control through deliberate undertakings that alter and distort our planet's delicate electromagnetic energy fields. However, instead of using this technology to destroy mankind, it now is clear that HAARP is being used to modify the weather to stop, or at least lessen, the effects of global warming in order to save mankind. Alternative 4 – the successor to Alternative 3 is now operational.

There is another factor now operating in conjunction with HAARP that has caught the attention of conspiracy writers around the world – the mystery of the "Chemtrails." It can now be revealed that this is the next phase of Alternative 4!

# The Lost Journals of Nikola Tesla

## The Mystery of the Chemtrails

We are all familiar with contrails, the exhaust left in the atmosphere by high-flying jet planes. Since 1997, observers all over the world have noticed an increase in these contrails with the skies being covered by a grid-pattern of high - altitude trails left by jets.

Active duty military personnel, police officers, pilots and defense specialists – as well as hundreds of everyday Americans quite used to seeing aircraft contrails and normal flight operations near cities, airports or over long-established routes, independently confirm the presence of multiple "lines in the sky" being purposefully laid by large jet tankers (usually white in color and always without identifying markings) over cities and rural areas.

As many as 20, 30 or more "contrails" are woven over hours into lattice-like grid patterns. "Tic-tac-toe in the sky" or "furrowing a farm field" are expressions commonly used to describe these multiple-aircraft maneuvers, in which white contrail-like emissions linger for hours, gradually spreading into a hazy overcast that completely obscures clear blue skies.

Normal contrails form when ice-crystals are disturbed by the passage of an airplane at high (cold) altitudes. Streaming from engines and wingtips, pencil-thin contrails almost always disappear within 45 seconds, fading quickly like the wake behind a boat.

While ice-crystal contrails can occasionally persist for hours, forming cirrus-type clouds that drift over a large area - particularly over high-traffic routes such as the Atlantic corridor between the USA and Europe - the chemtrails being reported daily by many independent eye-witnesses always linger for hours, forming an overcast from which veils of wispy fallout are often observed.

In some cases, commercial jetliners flying across these persistent grid-patterns lay normal contrails that disappear quickly alongside lingering chemtrails. Usually laid in an east-west direction, with characteristic X's and cris-cross trails also often observed, jets layering these deliberate chemtrails have often been observed switching their emissions off as they approach mountains or other geographically delineating features, only to turn their spray back on after making their turns back over the area being sprayed.

There has also been increased incidents of acute respiratory illness – including bronchitis, pneumonia and first-time asthma attacks in what doctors are calling epidemic levels across the USA and Great Britain. Fatalities, mostly among the elderly and immune-compromised, have exceeded 8,100 dead in England in the last week of December and first two weeks of January, 1999 according to the BBC.

Other observers report spraying from black, unmarked helicopters and twin-turboprop aircraft flying at rooftop level, often but not always at night. Incidents of chemicals being dumped from unmarked helicopters into municipal reservoirs have also been reported.

While chemtrail sightings have attracted strident attacks for lack of proof, videotape clearly shows billowing white spray being emitted from the tails of jets with wing-mounted engines, as well as from the wing sections outboard of the engines and inboard of the wingtips. These are the precise locations of wing- and tail-mounted refueling probes on tanker aircraft.

## The Spraying of America — A Brief History

In the closing months of World War II, a small task force of U. S. Naval ships maneuvered off the coast of southern California. Their objective was to gain information that military officers hoped would save thousands of American lives. Instead, this little excursion cost a few hundred innocent lives in the name of national security.

The expedition was the result of a fear among both Army and Navy officers that a super-secret Japanese military unit might be preparing to douse the West Coast with deadly bacteria. Ostensibly, a Japanese army "water purification" section situated in Pingfan, Manchuria – the group known as Unit 731 – actually was using prisoners, including Americans, as human guinea pigs in an effort to develop deadly toxins to destroy Japan's enemies.

In late 1941, the Japanese experimented with germ warfare by airdropping plague-infested materials over Changde, in China's Hunan Province. Later in the war, they began experimenting with large balloons, capable of carrying an incendiary bomb across the Pacific, by harnessing upper wind currents. The balloons were designed to fall on America, where the loss of gas brought them to Earth. By March 1945, more than 100 such balloons were known to have made their way to America through the jet stream.

# The Lost Journals of Nikola Tesla

The balloons landed as far north as White Horse, Alaska, and as far east as Grand Rapids, Michigan. In Oregon, six fishermen were killed when an incendiary-laden balloon exploded as they inspected it. Due to military secrecy, no one was warned of the balloon danger.

Military authorities feared that the worse was yet to come. They worried about the possibility of Unit 731 deploying balloons to release plague or encephalitis germs over America. Such concern led to high-level meetings in March 1945. Military authorities realized that a disaster could be caused by even one balloon releasing deadly biological agents.

What these officers needed to know was how fast and in which direction such diseases might travel – the so-called "vector" of the contagion. Navy ships were dispatched to steam along the coast of southern California, where, utilizing an early-morning mist as cover, sailors opened pressurized tanks filled with influenza virus. The contagion drifted ashore where other military men kept close tabs on both the speed and direction of infection.

Hospitals were monitored as far inland as 250 miles. More than 200 persons died in this flu outbreak, but the U. S. military got the information they wanted. Luckily the war ended before Japan could use their high-flying balloons to deliver deadly toxins to America. But U.S. government-led testing on its own civilian population continued well into the 1950s.

The army reportedly released simulant agents over hundreds of populated areas around the country. Targets included portions of Hawaii and Alaska, San Francisco, St. Louis, Minneapolis, New York City, Washington, D.C., Key West, Fort Wayne, Indiana and many other cities. The purpose was to see how the bacteria spread and survived as people went about their normal activities. No one learned of this secret experimentation for years because of top secret "national security."

In fact, during 45 years of open air testing, from time to time the army has stopped using certain simulants for reasons of safety. In each instance the army belatedly recognized they could be causing disease and death, although such information had long been available in the medical literature.

This was the case in the 1950s when it ceased using the fungus Aspergillus fumigatus as a simulant. The fungus had long been known to cause aspergillosis, a disease that can be fatal. Similarly, in the 1960s the army stopped using zinc cadmium sulfide, a chemical that had been known for years to cause cancer.

# The Lost Journals of Nikola Tesla

In the 1970s, the bacterium Serratia marcescens, a source of infections that can lead to death, was taken out of service as a simulant. In the 1980s, dimethyl methylphosphonate, a chemical known as DPP, was removed from use as a simulant because of its carcinogenic and other toxic potential.

Simulants in use today continue to pose risks. The chemical ethylene oxide, which is present in some of the mixtures used in outdoor spraying, is a known carcinogen. The bacterium Bacillus subtilis, while not generally seen as dangerous, is cited in medical textbooks as able to cause serious infections. Microorganism that seem harmless under some circumstances may cause illness under others.

Exposure to high concentrations of any microorganism can be critically dangerous to people in weakened conditions. The elderly, the very young, people with AIDS and others who have weakened immune systems are more susceptible to life threatening infections. Nevertheless, the army has not monitored the health of citizens who may have been exposed during its tests while maintaining that its bacterial agents cause no harm.

There could be two things that are going on with the chemtrials: Weather modification involving dangerous chemicals, and biowarfare experiments involving lab-produced pathogens. It could very well be that the characteristic X's in the sky are read by satellite to track dispersal patterns.

Weather is all about heat exchange. Heat generation can be artificially induced in the atmosphere by adding magnetic iron oxide powder to the polymer - and then heating it with HAARP or a more localized source. Bernard Eastlund, HAARP's inventor and original patent-holder, has said that this is theoretically possible - and that polymer additives for microwave absorption are commercially available.

Subsequent analysis by a private lab determined that some chemtrails contained a "strange ironlike substance." Chemtrail investigator Tommy Farmer comments that the chemist he engaged to examine an "angel hair" sample under a powerful microscope "noticed manmade yellow orange orbs impregnated into the filaments of the material." Farmer now believes this material could have been "oxidizing ferrous alloy" used in weather modification experiments.

Weather modification using chemtrails and other methods may be taking place across America without the help of HAARP, which according to Dr. Nick Begich (co-author of *Angels Don't Play This HAARP*) is apparently being activated only for short periods a few times a year.

# The Lost Journals of Nikola Tesla

A specialist who spoke under conditions of anonymity says that if HAARP "has anything to do with the contrails, I now realize we are talking about an altitude in the range of 10 Km. I don't know if it is possible to create [a resonance] region so close to the ground. None of the patents I have looked at are claiming anything less than 50 km. Furthermore, at the 10 Km height, it is hard to see how HAARP would have anything to do with effects seen in the lower 48 states or anywhere else on the planet."

When this engineer looked at other military applications for spraying organic electrolytes into the atmosphere, his patent searches turned up attempts to achieve over-the-horizon communications by reflecting radio waves off sprayed aerosols. "I could see that for over-the-horizon communications, one might make a reflector out of a grid pattern or parallel lines." Another patent shows a radar-jamming spray.

However, another weather modification expert insists that just as in shortwave radio, it is possible to use the ionosphere to "skip" HAARP radio-frequency transmissions to any region of the United States. Uncovered documents show that the Pentagon is also extremely interested in "steering storm systems" for weather modification, and in using sprayed aerosols to obscure the sky.

Chemtrail researcher Will Thomas agrees that the spraying seems to be for weather modification and/or neutralizing global warming effects. He further purports that this weather modification is being conducted due to pressure from insurance companies who see financial ruin on their horizon with continued high disaster-related claims. The catch? These weather modification tactics are further depleting the ozone hole and enhancing global warming. It is a short-term, "band-aid" answer with even worse consequences.

Spraying is generally done by certain planes: KC-10A, KC-135 (707) and C-130 for the high altitude spraying and C-130 turboprop aircraft for the low-level spraying. The KC-10A is a three-engine aircraft and would normally leave three parallel contrails in its wake.

The KC-135 is a smaller, four-engine aircraft that would typically display four parallel contrail lines. When used during chemtrail missions; however, these aircraft lay down only a single, thick, billowy chemtrail while simultaneously displaying no normal contrails. There are other planes which have been used in the spraying, but these are the main ones. Two types of spraying are done: high altitude meaning 20,000 feet and above and low altitude spraying.

# The Lost Journals of Nikola Tesla

## The Composition of Chemtrails

Part of the substances in the chemtrails have been identified: a cocktail of JP8+100 jet fuel, laced with Ethylene Dibromide (EDB). This chemical pesticide was banned in 1983 by the EPA as a definite carcinogen and chemical toxin. Exposure to this type spraying can include these symptoms: respiratory tract problems, severe infections to the throat and sinuses, swelling of the lymph glands, coughing fits, shortness of breath, sinus headaches, general respiratory failure, damage to the heart and liver, exposure to EDB makes people more susceptible to other biological agents due to severe lung irritation.

For lack of a better term, "brown goo" has been used to describe the material found on exterior walls of buildings and windshields of automobiles. It's almost impossible to remove with soap and water, and has proved to be highly toxic to anyone coming in contact with it.

Numerous red and white blood cells, and unidentified cell types have been found within the sub-micron fiber sample previously presented and submitted by Carol M. Browner, Administrator of the United States Environmental Protection Agency. The cells appear to be of a freeze-dried or desiccated nature in their original form within the microscopic fibers.

It has also been reported that spraying samples have been analyzed and have revealed that many deadly and toxic pathogens have been found including Mycoplasma Fermetens Incognitus. This is the same bioengineered pathogen that Dr. Garth Nicholson discovered in about 45% of the veterans who came down with Gulf War Illness.

Based on their published agenda, it is known that the US Air Force is currently engaged in extensive weather modification and control techniques in cooperation with Alternative 4. The Air Force also admits to "routine fuel dumping" of highly toxic JP8, and to using carbon black for weather modification. According to a recent NASA cloud study, carbon black is a "very effective" nuclei around which water vapor can condense, forming an artificially induced cloud cover.

Tommy Farmer, a former engineering technician with Raytheon Missile Systems, has been tracking patterns of jet contrails phenomena for more than a year. Farmer has "positively identified" two of the aircraft most often involved in the aerial spraying incidents as a Boeing KC-135 and Boeing KC-10. Both big jets are used by the US Air Force for air to air refueling.

Confirming reports from eye-witnesses across the United States, Farmer reports that all aircraft are painted either solid white or solid black with the exception of two KC-135s which are in training colors – orange and white. No identifying markings are visible.

Farmer has collected samples of what he calls "angel hair" sprayed by the mystery aircraft on six occasions since February, 1998. Four samples have been taken since November, 1998. Farmer says that globular filaments resembling ordinary spider webs, "usually fall in clumps or wads ranging from pencil eraser size to the size of a balled up fist."

Winds often whip the cobweb-like material into filaments as long as 50 feet. Farmer says that the sticky substance "melts in your hands" and adheres to whatever it touches. He also urges caution to collectors after becoming ill after his first contact with the angel hair. Farmer's ensuing sore throat and sinus infection lasted several months.

After repeatedly observing aircraft spraying particulates in front of and into cloud systems, Farmer is fairly certain the contrail phenomena is one part of a military weather modification system, possibly to slow down global warming. He notes that because the chemical contrails allow much more moisture to form inside cloud systems, severe localized storms result from the aerial seeding while surrounding areas that have surrendered their moisture to the storm cells experience drought.

In a U.S. Air Force research study, *Weather As A Force Multiplier*, issued in August, 1996, seven U.S. military officers outlined how HAARP and aerial cloud-seeding from tankers could allow U.S. Aerospace forces to "own the weather" by the year 2025. Among the desired objectives were "Storm Enhancement," "Storm Modification" and "Induce Drought."

According to the Air Force report, "In the United States, weather-modification will likely become a part of national security policy with both domestic and international applications."

Within 30 years, the Air Force foresees using Weather Force Support Elements with "the necessary sensor and communication capabilities to observe, detect, and act on weather-modification requirements to support U.S. military objectives" by "using airborne cloud generation and seeding" techniques being developed today. Other routine weather-modification missions will deploy "cirrus shields" formed by the chemical contrails of high-flying aircraft.

# The Lost Journals of Nikola Tesla

In 1966 Lyden, F.J. and Shipman, G.A. published their *Public Policy Issues raised by weather modification; possible alternative strategies for government action*: in Sewell, W.R.D., ed., Human Dimensions of Weather Modification, University of Chicago, Dept. of Geography, Research Paper # 105, pp. 289-303: "Is weather modification a public function, analogous to military protection, postal service, or highway construction? Or is it a private, non-governmental function? If the latter, is it a private function vested with a public interest, as had been determined to be the case, for example, in rail or air transportation? ... Or is weather modification an ordinary, lawful business, subject only to reasonable regulation, as in the manufacture and sale of clothing? This view raises questions about property rights, i.e., who owns the clouds?"

As British scientist W. J Maunder commented in his book, *The Value Of The Weather* (London: Methuen & Co. Ltd, 1970) "At least in the United States weather modification as a public function does not simplify matters, for a considerable amount of private capital has already been invested in cloud seeding enterprises, and any proposal of a governmental monopoly would undoubtedly meet with strong opposition from such investors. Even if these objections could be overcome, additional questions arise, such as should the program be a Federal governmental operation, or one administered by the states with co-ordination, and perhaps partial financing, by the Federal government."

It is also possible that the government is trying to vaccinate its citizenry against Anthrax, Tularemia, Brucellosis, or all three. Currently anthrax is probably the greatest national threat currently facing our country as well as other countries. It is easy to manufacture, transport and deliver, plus death follows fairly quickly. The economic devastation projected from an anthrax attack is significant.

The technology exists for this type of DNA vaccine. Peoples' symptoms experienced after a chemtrail spraying are consistent with symptoms one would see produced by agents associated with the host bacteria used to deliver the vaccine. However, until a sample group of people is actually tested for immunity to anthrax, there is no proof that it protects conclusively against anthrax.

Besides its obvious tactical military applications, aerial-seeding of contrail-clouds aligned in HAARP's characteristic grid-patterns could be part of a secret U.S. government initiative (Alternative 4 ) to address the global weather crisis brought about by atmospheric warming. This Tesla-based technology unfortunately is only a temporary fix to the worldwide warming problem.

# The Lost Journals of Nikola Tesla

## Project Cloverleaf

Chemtrail researcher C.E. Carnicom received a letter in May, 2000 from an airline manager who said that he had information concerning the chemtrails. The manager stated that he works for an undisclosed airline in upper management.

"Airline companies in America have been participating in something called **Project Cloverleaf** for a few years now. The earliest date anyone remembers being briefed on it is 1998. I was briefed on it in 1999.

"The few airline employees who were briefed on Project Cloverleaf were all made to undergo background checks, and before we were briefed on it we were made to sign non-disclosure agreements, which basically state that if we tell anyone what we know we could be imprisoned.

"About twenty employees in our office were briefed along with me by two officials from some government agency. They didn't tell us which one. They told us that the government was going to pay our airline, along with others, to release special chemicals from commercial aircraft.

"When asked what the chemicals were and why we were going to spray them, they told us that information was given on a need-to-know basis and we weren't cleared for it. They then went on to state that the chemicals were harmless, but the program was of such importance that it needed to be done at all costs.

"When we asked them why didn't they just rig military aircraft to spray these chemicals, they stated that there weren't enough military aircraft available to release chemicals on such a large basis as needs to be done. That's why Project Cloverleaf was initiated, to allow commercial airlines to assist in releasing these chemicals into the atmosphere. Then someone asked why all the secrecy was needed.

"The government reps then stated that if the general public knew that the aircraft they were flying on was releasing chemicals into the air, environmentalist groups would raise hell and demand the spraying stop. Someone asked one of the G-men then if the chemicals are harmless, why not tell the public what the chemicals are and why we are spraying them?

"He seemed perturbed at this question and told us in a tone of authority that the public doesn't need to know what's going on, but that this program is in their best interests. He also stated that we should not tell anyone, nor ask any more questions about it. With that, the briefing was over.

# The Lost Journals of Nikola Tesla

"All documents in our office pertaining to Project Cloverleaf are kept in locked safes. Nobody is allowed to take these documents out of the office. Very few employees are allowed access to these documents, and they remain tight-lipped about what the documents say.

"Mr. Carnicom, I am no fool. I know there's something going on. And frankly, I am scared. I feel a high level of guilt that I have been aware of this kind of operation but unable to tell anyone. It's been eating away at me, knowing that the company I work for may be poisoning the American people."

## The Governments Assessment of Devastating Climatic Changes

A coalition of U.S. government agencies unveiled in June 2000 the first national assessment on the potential consequences of climate change over the next 100 years, revealing a wide range of impacts if the Earth continues to warm significantly. Cold winters in the Northeast could become a thing of the past, alleviating some health stresses, the nation's food supply should be safe, and forests may proliferate.

However, at the same time, there will be drought concerns in every region of the United States, maple syrup will not flow easily in New England, and ecosystems may disappear entirely. Sources with environmental organizations who helped draft the assessment said the project offers a slew of scenarios for how the United States will be affected by a projected temperature rise of 5-10 degrees Fahrenheit by the year 2100.

Dr. Janine Bloomfield, an expert with the Environmental Defense organization in New York City, said the report is not final and will be open for public comment. "There are specifics on the impact on ecosystems, as well as the rate and magnitude of climate change," Bloomfield said.

The assessment breaks down how regions and specific sectors could be hurt or helped if the Earth warms at the same rate it has in recent years due to the accumulation of greenhouse gases in the atmosphere. It was written by a panel of scientists from several government agencies, academics, private groups, and other interested people ranging from farmers to fishermen.

According to the draft, the country must be prepared for the changes ahead, even if the exact impacts remain uncertain at this point. "It is very likely that some aspects and impacts of climate change will be totally unanticipated as complex systems respond to ongoing climate change in unforeseeable ways," it says.

Even if steps were taken in the near-term to reduce human greenhouse gas emissions, the report says, the level of gases already in the atmosphere will leave the world susceptible to climate change for the next century. "Even if the world takes mitigation measures, we must still adapt to a changing climate," the draft reports. "Similarly, even if we take adaptation measures, future emissions will have to be curbed to stabilize climate. Neither type of response can completely supplant the other."

An international attempt to tackle climate change, the Kyoto Protocol, has not been finished but it aims to reduce sharply the amount of fossil-fuel emissions from major industrial nations to 1990 levels by the years 2010-2012.

The following are some of the key findings listed in the assessment draft.

- Increased warming. Assuming continued growth in world greenhouse gas emissions, the climate models used in the assessment project that temperatures in the United States will rise 5-10 degrees Fahrenheit on average in the next 100 years.

- Differing regional impacts. Climate change will vary widely across the United States. Heavy and extreme precipitation events are likely to become more frequent, yet some regions will get drier.

- Vulnerable ecosystems. A few ecosystems such as alpine meadows in the Rocky Mountains and some barrier islands are likely to disappear entirely, while others such as forests in the Southeast are likely to experience major species shift or breakup. The goods and services lost through the disappearance or fragmentation of certain ecosystems are likely to be costly or impossible to replace.

- Widespread water concerns. Drought is an important concern in every region. Floods and water quality are also concerns. Snowpack changes are especially important in the West, Pacific Northwest and Alaska.

- Secure food supply. U.S. crop productivity is very likely to increase over the next few decades, but the gains will not be uniform across the nation. Falling prices and competitive pressures are very likely to stress some farmers.

- Forest productivity is likely to increase in some areas as trees respond to higher carbon dioxide levels. Climate change will also cause long-term shifts in forest species, such as sugar maples moving north out of the country.

The southeastern states could experience rising sea levels and more frequent storm surges threatening coastal development. Some coastal wetlands, barrier islands and beaches will disappear. The variety of tree species will increase, but many forests will be displaced by grassland and savannas. There could be an increase in water quality problems.

The northeastern states may see more warming that will ease winter weather extremes, but bring more rain and possible flooding. Warming may exacerbate pollution from agricultural runoff in places like the Chesapeake Bay. Hotter summers are likely, with more frequent and intense heat waves especially affecting cities. Forest species shift northward and maple trees may disappear. Some coastal urban centers may have to rework sewer, water and transportation systems because of sea level rise. Mountain regions will see a decline in skiing and increase in other activities such as hiking.

The great lakes states will experience a decline in water levels because of increased evaporation, leading to reduced water supply. Shoreline damage is likely to decrease, but lower water levels add to marine transportation problems. Cities along lakes must adapt to new water levels.

The Midwestern-great plains states may see increased stress in major cities because of extreme summer heat, but winters will become milder, reducing winter-related illnesses and deaths. Longer growing season and increases in carbon dioxide will cause higher crop yields and allow planting of more types of crops and in many cases more than one crop a year.

Despite higher rainfall, warmer weather will increase evaporation, reducing lake and river water levels. Likelihood of more droughts and flash flooding. Farming on marginal land will become more difficult. Western and Mountain States could see warmer winter temperatures that will reduce snow accumulations in mountains, reducing summer runoff and complicating water management, flood control and irrigation. Higher elevation ecosystems will shift with parts of the mountain region becoming drier. Alpine meadows in the Rocky Mountains are likely to face extreme stress and may disappear.

Southwestern states could face increased moisture which will result in a decline of desert ecosystems, while shrub lands expand. Increase in crop diversity. Areas may have a variation of wet and dry periods adding to flooding and fire risks. Some birds and mammals may shift to higher elevations, while reptiles and amphibians may move to lower elevations with warming. Changes in mountain snowpack will require changes in water management.

Warmer water temperatures may cause some fish species, including Pacific Northwest salmon, to migrate northward in the northwestern states and Alaska. Warmer water species may move into the Northwest. Warmer weather is likely to increase rainfall in the summer and cause changes in species mix. Sea level rise will impact low-lying areas, especially in Puget Sound area. Warming in Alaska will increase permafrost thawing, resulting in damage to roads, buildings and impacting forests.

Islands all over the planet will have to face rising sea levels and increased possibility of storms. This may reduce availability of fresh water and in some cases pose health risks. Higher water temperatures and increased carbon dioxide levels are likely to exacerbate coral bleaching and increase destruction of coral reefs off southern Florida and Hawaii Islands.

Science and environmental groups lauded the draft as a "balanced assessment" of the potential impacts of climate variability and change on the United States but warned that unless the nation saw the report as a "wake up call," nothing good would come from its release. In a joint statement from Environmental Defense, National Environmental Trust, Natural Resources Defense Council, Union of Concerned Scientists and the World Wildlife Fund, the groups said it was time to take climate change seriously.

A top secret government report that will not be released to the public, confirms the climate assessment report, but adds that due to the difficulties of finding a worldwide solution to increased air pollution, global warming will continue to increase beyond the five to ten degrees postulated by current analysis. The report continues with an estimate that the planet's temperature will likely increase twenty to thirty degrees within one hundred years, making human life impossible.

**Aircraft, tentatively identified as an MD-80, leaves a trail of chemicals that could be used in conjunction with HAARP to modify global warming.**

# Conclusions

Even though several years have passed, Dale Alfrey continues to try and recover his lost Tesla notes. He feels that somewhere there exists additional papers and notes, perhaps forgotten in someone's basement or attic. Alfrey has spent a number of hours scouring the Internet seeking people who may have the information he is looking for. Unfortunately, nothing has been found.

It is certain that other missing Tesla documents are still "out there somewhere." According to the book: *Tesla – Man Out of Time*, in 1928, Tesla's friend, John O'Neill happened to see a legal advertisement in a New York newspaper announcing that six boxes placed in storage by Tesla would be sold by the storage warehouse for unpaid bills. Feeling that such material should be preserved, O'Neill went to Tesla and asked permission to try and obtain funds to reclaim the material.

"Tesla hit the ceiling," he recalled. "He assured me he was well able to take care of his own affairs. He forbid me to buy them or do anything in any way about them."

Shortly after the inventor died, O'Neill got in touch with Sava Kosanovic, told him about the boxes, and urged him to protect them. He was never able to get a positive statement from Kosanovic that he had obtained the boxes and examined the contents. "He gave evasive assurances that there was no reason for me to worry."

Despite the incomplete notes that Tesla left behind, Alfrey thinks that he has been able to put together a rough idea of what Tesla was researching and why. Some of these notes were Tesla's work in vertical take-off and landing (VTOL) aircraft, strange drawings of unusual vehicles, reactive jet dirigibles and hovercraft and also combination helicopter/airplanes that the inventor designed. Clearly, Tesla is one of the forefathers of both the Harrier jet, which can hover and take off vertically, and the Osprey helicopter-airplane.

After his initial Colorado Springs experiments in 1899, Tesla started experimenting with better radio transmitters and receivers in order to repeat his reception of the anomalous signals he picked up in Colorado. Tesla considered his methods of reception and transmission utilized not Hertzian waves, or what we now refer to as transverse electromagnetic waves (radio), but another type of signal transmission.

# The Lost Journals of Nikola Tesla

He described them as faster-than-light (FTL) longitudinal wave transmissions. Tesla may have been receiving on the ELF specturm (Extremely Low Frequencies). The ELF spectrum is below the 10 KHz. boundary of internationally regulated frequencies . It is usually considered to be the spectrum of 3 Hz. to 30 Hz. (VLF-3 to 30 KHz.) (ULF-300 to 3000 Hz.) (ELF-3 to 300Hz.). The wavelengths in the ELF range are from 100,000 Km. to 1,000 Km., and the wavelength for the earth's 40,000 Kms. circumference falls within that spread.

Tesla obviously succeeded to such a degree that he was soon receiving voice transmissions. These transmissions he speculated were originating from people on other worlds. Tesla gave a few public hints about these interplanetary transmissions, such as in 1937, he announced: "I have devoted much of my time during the year past to the perfecting of a new small and compact apparatus by which energy in considerable amounts can now be flashed through interstellar space to any distance without the slightest dispersion." (*New York Times*, Sunday, 11 July 1937)

A degree of confirmation of Tesla's interplanetary communications came from Arthur Mathews who claimed that Tesla had secretly developed the "Teslascope" for the purpose of communicating with Mars. Matthews' father was a laboratory assistant to the noted physicist Lord Kelvin back in the 1890s. Tesla once came over to England to meet Kelvin to convince him that Alternating Current was more efficient than Direct. When Matthews was 16 his father arranged for him to apprentice under Tesla. He eventually worked for him and continued this alliance until Tesla's death in 1943.

"It's not generally known, but Tesla actually had two huge magnifying transmitters built in Canada, and Matthews operated one of them. People mostly know about the Colorado Springs transmitters and the unfinished one on Long Island. I saw the two Canadian transmitters. All the evidence is there.

"The Teslascope is the thing Tesla invented to communicate with beings on other planets. In principle, it takes in cosmic ray signals and eventually the signals are stepped down to audio. Speak into one end, and the signal goes out the other end as a cosmic ray emitter."

With the exception of Matthews statements, there has been no concrete evidence that Tesla managed to communicate with extraterrestrials or whoever was transmitting to Tesla's ELF receiver. It seems that Tesla was on the receiving end only. Nevertheless, Tesla managed to glean a substantial amount of good information from these transmissions, enough to influence his research and inventions for the remaining forty three years of his life.

It was during this period that Tesla found himself ostracized by most of the scientific community. His efforts to interest others in such wild inventions as free-energy, beam weapons, wireless power transmissions, antigravity devices, anti-war shields, resonation and a plethora of others, no doubt led to him being considered a crackpot. Sadly, Tesla had become the apodeme of a mad scientist.

Yet, it was obvious that his letters to the government and military had aroused some interest. A young American engineer engaged in war work consulted Tesla on a ballistics engineering problem because he could not get time on an overworked computer, and Tesla's mind was known to offer the nearest thing to it. Soon he became fascinated with Tesla's scientific papers and was allowed to take batches of them home to his hotel room where he and another American engineer pored over them each night. They were returned the next day, a procedure which continued for about two weeks prior to Tesla's death.

Tesla had received offers to work for Germany and Russia. After the inventor died, both engineers became concerned that critical scientific information had fallen into foreign hands and alerted United States security agencies and high government officials.

Just how much of Tesla's work remains hidden in the top secret bowels of the military is unknown. It can be deduced that Tesla's theories of extraterrestrials and global warming were taken seriously by some in high-levels of authority, because it is now known that the United States government and military were the first to give credence that UFOs were spacecraft from other planets.

It is interesting to note that between 1945 and 1948 an exchange of letters and cables occurred among the Air Technical Service Command at Wright Field in Dayton, Ohio, Military Intelligence in Washington, and the Office of Alien Property. The subject? Files of the late Nikola Tesla.

On September 5, 1945, Colonel Holliday of the Equipment Laboratory, Propulsion and Accessories Subdivision, wrote to Lloyd L. Shaulis of the OAP in Washington, confirming a conversation and asking for photostatic copies of the notes and papers of the late Tesla. It was stated that the material would be used "in connection with projects for national defense by this department."

Shaulis made the material available to Air Technical Service Command, but there is no record of how many copies were sent. Nor was the material ever returned. These were full photostatic copies, not merely the abstracts. The Navy has no record of Tesla's papers; no federal archives have records of them.

Four months after the photostats had been sent to Wright Field, Col. Ralph Doty, the chief of Military Intelligence in Washington wrote James Markham of Alien Property indicating that they had never been received: "This office is in receipt of a communication from Headquarters, Air Technical Service Command, Wright Field, requesting that we ascertain the whereabouts of the files of the late scientist, Dr. Nikola Tesla, which may contain data of great value to the above Headquarters. It has been indicated that your office might have these files in custody. If this is true, we would like to request your consent for a representative of the Air Technical Service Command to review them. In view of the extreme importance of these files to the above command, we would like to request that we be advised of any attempt by any other agency to obtain them.

"Because of the urgency of this matter, this communication will be delivered to you by a Liaison Officer of this office in the hope of expediting the solicited information."

The "other" agency that had the files, or should have had them, was the Air Technical Service Command itself. On October 24, 1947, David L. Bazelon, assistant attorney general and director of the Office of alien Property, wrote to the commanding officer of the Air Technical Service Command regarding the Tesla photostats. They had not been returned and the OAP wanted them back.

Obviously at least one set of Tesla's papers had reached Wright Field because on November 25, 1947, there was a response to the Office of Alien Property from Colonel Duffy, chief of the Electronic Plans Section, Electronic Subdivision, Engineering Division, Air Material Command, Wright Field. He replied: "These reports are now in the possession of the Electronic Subdivision and are being evaluated. This should be completed by January 1, 1948. At that time your office will be contacted with respect to final disposition of these papers." They were never returned or even acknowledged to have ever existed at all!

In response to a Freedom of Information Act request in 1980, Wright - Patterson Air Force base stated: "The organization (Equipment Laboratory) that performed the evaluation of Tesla's papers was deactivated several years ago. After conducting an extensive search of lists of records retired by that organization, in which we found no mention of Tesla's papers, we concluded the documents were destroyed at the time the laboratory was deactivated."

# The Lost Journals of Nikola Tesla

## Afterthoughts on Nikola Tesla, Alien Among Us
## By Diane Tessman

Nikola Tesla was an alien in a tough, cruel world. He was a gentle, humble man and the gaudy objects which money can buy, did not impress him in the least. He was out of place and out of time. And he was brilliant! No one since has equaled him in sheer scientific creativity and genius.

Tesla disliked the compromises, greed, and lies of "big business" in his day. Just think how much worse it has gotten today. Many of us feel as Tesla did, but the individual's lone voice echos in a vast wasteland. We may keep our soul, as Tesla did, but we also feel like aliens in this greedy world.

Tesla possessed integrity, dignity, and an innate sense of fair play. Injustice made him furious. However, if his amazing inventions were to be used by large corporations in promoting electrical energy and his other unique scientific innovations, he would have to bend to their self-serving ways. He did not!

He suffered greatly for his stand against big business and greed. He was virtually homeless, living in fleabag hotels, and had to watch as others became wealthy and famous for inventions which were not the equal of his; some highly successful technology was directly stolen from him. Tesla lived in poverty and anonymity but he kept his integrity. His soul was his own.

W.B. Yeats writes of a "pioneer soul" and this term applies to Nikola Tesla. He was an individual ahead of his time; even today, he would find the world greedy, ignorant and cruel. He belongs to the future, a time when humankind will learn to feel, think and act on a higher, more enlightened level. He belongs to the future day when we will indeed do unto others, as we would have them do unto us.

Many seekers of truth, both scientific and metaphysical, have been drawn to Nikola Tesla. He speaks to us. We are awed at his inventions and knowledge, and we are inspired by his gentle enlightenment and strength of character. Tesla possesses an immortal, mysterious persona which intrigues anyone who does not accept anything at face value.

Albert Einstein felt that true scientific genius is based in the mystical world; as we are drawn to Tesla and as he speaks to us, we perceive this truth again: Tesla's scientific brilliance has its foundation in the spiritual and the mystical.

I have been a channel for 18 years and have received transmissions from a variety of interdimensional beings. At this time, Nikola Tesla sent through me, the following message for humanity as the new millennium dawns across the face of the planet: "Humankind, this is the being you know as Tesla. I greet you in the light of good intent. I am no longer in that "Tesla" physical form, having gone on many of your Earth years ago, to a different world in Space/Time. I am happy here; I am home.

"I came to your world, as you did, to make it a better place. You may have lost sight temporarily of the fact that you came to Earth to make it a better place. Why? Because you are so busy just trying to survive there. You are fatigued much of the time, and speaking of time – it just flies by! I had this problem as well, and there were many times when I felt lost and depressed. But I did live my human lifetime to help enlightened its people, and you have also chosen this path.

"If you can leave your problems for a moment, and fly above the trees, you will see Earth and your lifetime there in a clear perspective. Your higher perspective of "the forest" tells you that you are there for a reason – to make a difference.

"Do not lose your integrity, therefore. Gather your dignity about you, and never stop having that sense of fair play. Your power base is within yourself, not in the big corporations which attempt to run your life. They can never own you if you keep possession of your soul. They can never control your mind if you continue to allow your mind to be free and enlightened.

"The time is soon coming when "their" day will be over! The big international corporations are not eternal. Their greedy, cruel ways selfishly trouncing on other humans, on nature's creatures, on the environment, and on the planet herself, will soon come to an end.

"Our day is coming, my fellow pioneer soul. My spirit, my persona hovers around Earth in these days, assisting you when and where I can. This is partially why you feel intrigued with my character and my work. I attempt to channel messages to budding inventors and scientists, and I attempt to inspire spiritual seekers as well.

"A new dawn comes, and a world emerges in which we are not aliens. The vibrations of gentleness, enlightenment, curiosity, integrity and justice will be, THE WAY IT IS. I thank you for you interest. (Transmission from) TESLA."

* You can write to Diane Tessman at P.O. Box 352, St. Ansgar, Iowa, 50472. Ask for a free *Star Network Heartline* newsletter. You can also log onto Diane's Star People Homesite on the Internet: http://www.members.tripod.com/starpeople

If you have any information on the whereabouts of other "lost" boxes of Nikola Tesla's notes and journals – Please E-mail your story to the *Conspiracy Journal* at this address: commanderx12@hotmail.com

You can also send a regular letter to:

Global Communications
P.O. Box 753
New Brunswick, NJ 08903

Be sure to visit the Conspiracy Journal website at: http://www.webufo.net for all the news and information that everyone else is too afraid to print.

# TESLA'S "LOST" INVENTIONS AND THE SECRET
# OF THE PURPLE HARMONY GENERATORS

Upon the passing of Nikola Tesla, huge boxes containing his private journals and unpatented inventions were retained by the Custodian of Alien Properties and were locked away. From inside information gathered in the years following his death, it was ascertained that officials from Wright-Patterson Air Force Base (also the home for many years of Project Blue Book, headquarters of the government's UFO cover-up attempt) hurried to the warehouses of the Custodian of Alien Properties and took possession of all of Tesla's documents and other materials, all of which were classified at the highest level. To this day, a great deal of Tesla's papers remain in government hands and are still highly classified. There are literally tons of notes, documents, drawings, and plans, as well as over twenty boxes of reportedly "missing" Tesla material. The government distributed false rumors that Tesla never kept notes, which is a blatant lie.

Over the course of time -- largely in the last decade -- some of Tesla's lost journals have been uncovered, and a number of his "secret inventions" have been privately developed. One of these inventions is Tesla's Purple Harmony Generator -- also know as Tesla's Purple Energy Plate. Though the "generators" have been around for a number of years, they are only now starting to receive the international attention they deserve in the alternative energy field. In an article published in the August 2000 edition of the popular FATE magazine, author Corrie DeWinter mentions that she first became aware of the generators while reading a book called STAR SIGNS by Linda Goodman. "Goodman mentions that the person who created the plates with Tesla preferred to remain anonymous. However, after the inventor's death, the company which produced the plates decided to give him due credit. The inventor, Ralph Bergstresser was born in 1912 in Pueblo, Colorado, of German parents who immigrated to the United States. He was extremely interested in free energy, or Zero Point Energy" as it is now called in scientific circles. Bergstresser carefully studied anything written about Nikola Tesla's experiments, and attended many lectures given by Tesla. At one point they were introduced and quickly became friends, due to their shared interest in free energy."

According to the FATE article, Bergstresser continued with his work for many years and following Tesla's death came into possession of several notebooks which helped him further develop the harmony plates. For all intents and purposes the plates look innocent enough. Coming in a variety of sizes, they are purple in color and are said to be "in resonance, or in tune, with the basic energy of the universe. They function as transceivers...creating a field of energy around themselves that will penetrate any material substance by osmosis. The energy is very beneficial to all life...plant, animal, or human. It might be considered as Positive Energy." Somehow or other -- according to current thinking regarding the plates -- the original atoms of the anodized aluminum structures are restructured when put through a proprietary process whereby the vibrational frequency of the atoms and electrons is changed.

Non-approved FDA testing has reportedly shown that the healing process is accelerated for burns and bone fractures when the injured party becomes the focal point of the purple plates' force field by wearing one of the self contained generators. Aches and pains are said to go away, the quality of sleep may be improved, water and food becomes more tasty (to establish this simply put a purple plate on a shelf in your frig. The quality of cheap wine is remarkably enhanced. Plates have been placed under sick houseplants, and near the food dish of small pets. Corrie De Winter in her FATE article offers several suggestions for the use of the plates: "Place a small-size plate in a pocket or purse for energy...small plate (is often) placed on forehead to alleviate headache pain, on joints to alleviate gout and arthritis pain, on stomach to stop nausea...Placed on forehead in the morning will help you to remember your dreams...I have also read testimonials from plate users who claim they help with cramps, headaches, stomach upsets, stiff joints, torticollis, swelling, ringworm, 'clicking' jaw, alcoholism, anxiety, colic and depression."

Probably one of the most influential tests has been conducted by the Perrysburg School District allowing them to stop using dangerous pesticides around the Frank Elementary School pupils and very naturally by utilizing the Tesla generators or plates. According to the school custodian, the plates where installed in the cafeteria and elsewhere around the building allowing them to greatly control the pest population. One of the most commonly used pesticides was developed by Hitler in World War II to penetrate mustard gas masks...the purple plates provide a totally safe means to attack the problem of pests. Tesla's Purple Harmony Plates come in a number of sizes and are now available through the publishers of this special insider report (see next page). Test them yourself!

# Enjoy the Technology of TOMORROW Today!

## ● TESLA PURPLE ENERGY PLATES

Now you can test for yourself the power of the unseen energy forces trapped inside of the Purple Energy Plates. These plates are in no way harmful. They can be placed directly on the skin, put in your refrigerator, carried in your pocket, worn, placed in any room of the house.

Several sizes are available:
LARGE PLATES (12"x12")  $45.00 or 3 for $120.00        (For inside refrigerators, around house, etc)
SMALL PLATES (2 3/4" x 4 1/2")  $22.95 or 3 for $60.00    (Good for under pillow, near plants, pet disc, etc)
ENERGY DISCS (1.5")  $15 or 3 for $35.00   (Ideal to carry)

Note: Add $4 for shipping

## SUGGESTED VIEWING --
## ■ FREE ENERGY AND ANTI-GRAVITY

90 minutes  VHS  Hosted by Tom Valone   $25.00

Now at the start of a new millennium, new technologies are emerging that create "Free Energy" (electricity without an electric bill), "Free Propulsion" (drive for miles without paying for fuel) and "ANTI GRAVITY" (leaving the surface of the road while you are driving).

With diagrams, pictures and video clips, this report has been presented before large audience many times by physicist, engineer, author and college professor, Thomas Valone, M.A., PE.

Valone's captivating style will astound you with the truth about electrogravitics, inertial propulsion, free energy, magnetic motors, N-machines, the Searle effect, the Hutchinson effect, nuclear batteries and much more. Learn what these 21st Century technologies will allow you PERSONALLY to do. See demonstrations of anti-gravity and inertial propulsion that defies explanation. Become an expert on the new realities of free energy.

## ■ MIRACLE IN THE VOID        Add $4 to total order for shipping up to 3 tapes or books,
110 minutes  VHS  Hosted by Dr Brian O'Leary   $25.00                    $6 for larger orders!

One of the original astronauts, Dr O'Leary presents the latest evidence for the birth of a new science of consciousness, which can offer solutions to the ravages of pollution. At center stage is his report on the remarkable research for clean, cheap energy to replace fossil fuels, which could reverse abnormal changes in our climate.

Using a spoon bending demonstration as an example, O'Leary describes the interaction between science and spirit, of physics and metaphysics. He openly acknowledges the challenges many new science pioneers face through ridicule from vested interests, as expressed by his muppet alter ego called "the lapis pig." Dr. O'Leary offers hope for a paradigm shift which will help us restore Eden to earth. Brilliant presentation!

## SUGGESTED READING
## ■ INCREDIBLE TECHNOLOGIES OF THE NEW WORLD ORDER: UFOS, NIKOLA TESLA, AREA 51
## by Commander X   144 pgs   $15.00

Here is a fascinating update on the technologies being tested and actively used today by Big Brother. There is said to be an incredible array of electromagnetic transmitters currently in operation by the New World Order for the purposes of global mind control -- something Tesla faught against all his life.

## Global Communications, Box 753, New Brunswick, NJ 08903
Checks, money orders or credit card (VISA, MASTERCARD, DISCOVER) accepted. Do not send cash.
24 hour order hot line 732 602-3407 or e mails to MRUFO@webtv.net

Global Communications, Box 753, New Brunswick, NJ 08903

*THEORIES THAT ARE CLASSIFIED ABOVE TOP SECRET*

# NEW FROM INNER LIGHT PUBLICATIONS

# SECRET BLACK PROJECTS OF THE NEW WORLD ORDER

### by Tim Swartz

The author of this highly controversial book is Tim Swartz, an Emmy Award winning television producer who maintains that his research shows that all kinds of strange aircraft are flying overhead that may be based on back engineered alien technology (possibly the result of one or more UFO crash-landings).

"Reports of unusual aerial and ground level activity at high security places such as Area 51 are now ignored heavily due to the 'kook factor' often associated with UFOs by the press and other authorities. But for disinformation to be effective, it must contain some elements of truth. These black-budgeted aircraft—consisting of mysterious flying triangles—include anti-gravity and techniques of invisibility and are so highly sophisticated that the possibility exists that the science used could be the result of an exchange between earthly forces and alien intelligence." Includes information on various underground projects in the command of the sinister New World Order.

**ISBN: 0-938294-80-6 7x10 140 pages $12.95**

# EVIL AGENDA OF THE SECRET GOVERNMENT

## Exposing Project Paper Clip and the Underground UFO Bases of Hitler's Elite Scientific Corps

### by Tim Swartz

Because of the foreseeable threat of communism's spread after World War II, secret alliances were formed between certain elements of U.S. intelligence with German agents who slowly infiltrated the U.S. military, government and large corporations. Nearly 800 scientists were granted U.S. citizenship. At several locations (including what is now known as Area 51), German scientists started work on a radically different technology that most Americans would consider—out of this world! Some call it "Free Energy!"

In addition to "fancy flying machines," a fraction of the U.S. intelligence community worked with these relocated Nazi scientists on brainwashing techniques and biological warfare in order to control the American population should the need arise.

The Secret Government's New World Order plans total control and is using the manipulation of religion, genetic engineering, drugs and control of weather in their sinister plot. And while there are both good and bad aliens coming to Earth, the Secret Government would like to blame as much as possible on ETs to keep the unsuspecting public off their trail. If necessary they will use the idea of an "alien threat" to bring about "world unity" under their domination.

The author reveals that the real power behind the Secret Government is located in underground bases in the Antarctic, which has been dubbed the "Last Nazi Battalion." Many UFO abductees are brought to this local to be experimented upon. The New World Order has developed psychosurgery, implants and ESP to create the use of "screen memories" as UFO cover stories.

**ISBN: 1-892062-00-3 7x10 150 pages $14.95**